There are many current cultural myths regarding the process of grieving as well as the nature of loss. These include notions that change and loss can be avoided, grieving is something one should "get over," and that suffering has no purpose. *Capturing Shadows: Poetic Encounters Along the Path of Grief and Loss* shatter these and other misguided beliefs regarding dying and grieving in a creative and personally powerful way. By going beyond the usual intellectual attempts to alter our more accepted ways of seeing the world, poetic expression has the power to transform not just our usual way of knowing, but our very way of being-in-the-world. I encourage those who are open to being deeply affected and transformed regarding their present awareness of grief and loss to engage these encounters with an open and receptive heart. You will experience changing in a wiser and deeper way.

Ron Valle, PhD
Psychologist

Author of *Opening to Dying and Grieving: A Sacred Journey*

Capturing Shadows is an exquisite testimony to the healing power of poetry expressed in the raw experience of sharp grief and penetrating loss. Readers must prepare to have their defenses disarmed as tears take them again and again through the pain of these poets to transformational love and awe. This book will be cherished by all who have grieved and by all who accompany others as they heal from deep sorrow.

Sue Cooper, PhD
Psychologist

In his book *Love and Will*, Rollo May observed that artists do not provide us solutions but give us contributions that help us to remain resolute in our searching process. C.S. Lewis, the eminent theologian, shared that we read to know that we're not alone. This marvelous book offers us poetic expressions of grief and loss that can help dissolve our sense of alienation in the searching process that is part of all losses and transitions. I urge you to dive into the poetry within and discover for yourself the wisdom of the proverb that shared grief is half the grief while shared joy is twice the joy.

Mark Yang, PsyD
Director of the International Institute of Existential Humanistic Psychology; Adjunct Faculty & Director of Existential-Humanistic Programs in Asia, Saybrook University

This beautifully crafted book seeks to do nothing less than revolutionize our attitude toward an ancient means of dealing positively with the mystery of loss: poetry. It not only encourages us to put our own loss-related painful feelings and plaintive cries into writing but also to bond with others in their attempts to do so. Moving examples of everyday people's poems are followed by restorative activities we can perform, alone or with others, once our poems are brought to life. This calm, professional examination of the use of poetry as a means of healing enables teachers, mental health professionals, and spiritual guides—as well as those who seek their help—to transform death into life and pain into peace. This provocative book allows all who read it to learn in the non-threatening and freeing atmosphere that truly good teachers create.

Judith A. Schaeffer, PhD, OSF

Capturing Shadows is a collection of poems that I highly recommend to everyone, especially those of us who have survived tragedies or are looking to find the light out of the darkness for a better life. The words you will read of sadness, respect, hope, and love are truly moving and make you appreciate the time you have on this earth and with those whom you love. As a survivor of the 9/11 attacks, I identify with many of the poems and it is refreshing and comforting to read feelings that I have felt and had to deal with in the words of others. They are words that give me hope, love, and reflection of life, and that in itself makes *Capturing Shadows* priceless.

William Jimeno
9/11 survivor

In voices as variegated as the losses they describe, these poets write from the heart of grief for an audience of one--and through these published pages, to many. What emerges from their sometimes homespun, sometimes elegant verse is a rich quilt that captures the nuances of mourning in all of its lived complexity, offering a generous resource for the bereaved to explore—and using the toolbox of techniques provided by Hoffman and Moats—to express their personal trauma and transformation in poetry of their own. Bridging literary and therapeutic intents, the resulting anthology exemplifies what might appropriately be termed the "healing arts."

Robert A. Neimeyer, PhD
Editor of *Grief and the Expressive Arts: Practices for Creating Meaning*

Capturing Shadows:
Poetic Encounters Along the Path of Grief and Loss

Louis Hoffman
Michael Moats
Editors

University Professors Press
Colorado Springs, CO

Book Copyright © 2015
The authors of the poems retain the copyright for all poems in this book.

Capturing Shadows: Poetic Encounters Along the Path of Grief and Loss
By Louis Hoffman and Michael Moats

All rights reserved. No portion of this book may be reproduced by any process or technique without the express written consent of the publisher.

First Published in 2015, University Professors Press.

ISBN 13: 978-1-939686-09-1

University Professors Press
Colorado Springs, CO
www.universityprofessorspress.com

Front Photo by Michael Moats
Cover Design by Laura Ross

Dedication

I dedicate this book to my parents, Clarence and Lynn Hoffman. You have been more than my mother and my father; you have been mentors, inspirations, and a deep source of joy throughout my life, even when I resisted this recognition. If not for your love for me and the love for others I witnessed in you, this book would never have come into being.
~ Louis Hoffman

This book is dedicated to my mentors of living and dying that shared their gifts before leaving this world, as they refused to stop teaching. To those that have knowingly faced the end of their physical existence, to those that remained beside them, and to those that remained beside the bereaved, my contribution is for you. It is my hope that this collaborative book of experiences and expressions of loss and transition becomes a companion to those that feel helpless and those that enter their world with their own sense of helplessness and tolerate the discomfort of not doing, not fixing, and not being able to make things better, except through the willingness to continually share their limited and sacrificial presence.
~ Michael Moats

Poetry, Healing, and Growth Series

Stay Awhile: Poetic Narratives on Multiculturalism and Diversity
Louis Hoffman & Nathaniel Granger, Jr. (Eds.)

Capturing Shadows: Poetic Encounters Along the Path of Grief and Loss
Louis Hoffman & Michael Moats (Eds.)

Journey of the Wounded Soul: Poetic Companions for Spiritual Struggles
Louis Hoffman & Steve Fehl (Eds.)

Our Last Walk: Using Poetry for Grieving and Remembering Our Pets
Louis Hoffman, Michael Moats, and Tom Greening (Eds.)

Poems For and About Elders (Revised & Expanded Edition)
Tom Greening

Connoisseurs of Suffering: Poetry for the Journey to Meaning
Jason Dias & Louis Hoffman (Eds.)

Poetry, Healing, and Growth Series

Poetry is an ancient healing art used across cultures for thousands of years. In the Poetry, Healing, and Growth book series, the healing and growth-facilitating nature of poetry is explored in depth through books of poetry and scholarship, as well as through practical guides on how to use poetry in the service of healing and growth. Poetry written with an intention to transform suffering into an artistic encounter is often different in process and style from poetry written for art's sake. This series offers engagement with the poetic greats and literary approaches to poetry while also embracing the beauty of fresh, poetic starts and encouraging readers to embark upon their own journey with poetry. Whether you are an advanced poet, avid consumer, or novice to poetry, we are confident you will find something to inspire your thinking on your personal path toward healing and growth.

Series Editors,
Carol Barrett, PhD; Steve Fehl, PsyD; Nathaniel Granger, Jr, PsyD; Tom Greening, PhD; and Louis Hoffman, PhD

Table of Contents

Acknowledgements: A Testament to Meaning in Relationships	1
Setting the Context	5
Preface – Myrtle Heery	7
Foreword - Alan D. Wolfelt	9
Introduction	11
Opening – *Robert A. Neimeyer*	29
The Falling of Hair – *Carol Barrett*	30
I Had to Say Goodbye Tonight – *Louis Hoffman*	32
Two Balloons – *Michael Moats*	34
September 11 – *David N. Elkins*	36
Stupid Raven – *Ted Mallory*	40
Losing My Mind – *Nesreen Alsoraimi*	42
Moonless Night – *Juanita Ratner*	44
Passage of Sorrow – *Nance Reynolds*	46
Atonal Autumn – *Candice Hershman*	48
Watching Ants – *Tammy Nuzzo-Morgan*	50
Ode to Joseph – *Lisa Vallejos*	51
No Milk – *Louis Hoffman*	52
After My Death – *Carol Barrett*	53
Alchemy – *Wade Agnew*	54
Changed Lenses – *Michael Moats*	56
The Art of Longing – *Robert A. Neimeyer*	58
The Honeymoon is Over – *David Bentata*	60
The Day the Wild Horses – *Susan Gabrielle*	61
The Love of a Childless Mother – *Veronica Lac*	62
A Mother's Hug – *Michael Moats*	64
I Want to Be Ready – *Louis Hoffman*	65
Written on a Plane on the Inside Jacket of a Paperback on the way Home – *Ted Mallory*	66
A Happy Old Man – *Paul T. P. Wong*	67
Instructions for a Long Life – *Carol Barrett*	68
Blessed or Cursed – *Nesreen Alsoraimi*	69

13 – *LeesaMaree Bleicher*	71
Blanched – *Aarica Geitner*	73
Death Poem #13 – *Richard Bargdill*	74
Forever/Now – *Joel Federman*	75
Take My Hand – *Deerheart*	76
Breakfast at the Retreat – *Robert A. Neimeyer*	77
Desert Dreams – *Nesreen Alsoraimi*	78
Do You Have a Minute – *David Bentata*	80
Viscous Cycle – *Joy L. S. Hoffman*	82
Understanding Life in Death – *Emily Lasinsky*	84
Heal (Image) – *Emily Lasinsky*	85
Brown Chair – *Louis Hoffman*	86
Little Ones – *Alexandra O'Toole*	88
My Grandpa's Farm – *Ted Mallory*	89
Let Me Help You, Dad – *Michael Moats*	90
One Last Tear – *Nathaniel Granger, Jr.*	92
Kindergarten Doorway/Here and Not Here – *Larry Graber*	95
Go My Children – *Richard Bargdill*	100
Crow Party – *Susan Gabrielle*	103
Father – *Staci Fraley*	105
Flame Eternal – *Kat V. Rosemond*	107
My First Suicide – *Carol Barrett*	108
People in the Streets – *Louis Hoffman*	110
Pink Rain – *Paul T. P. Wong*	111
Lebkuchengewuerz – *Katherine Kreil-Sarkar*	112
Séance – *Nesreen Alsoraimi*	113
Seeing You Die and Letting You Go – *Monica Mansilla*	114
Melting Snow – *Michael Moats*	116
Hospital Haiku – *Tracy Lee Sisk*	119
An Ecology of Grief (Haiku Collection) – *Virginia (Gina) Subia Belton*	120
Nearness of You – *Louis Hoffman*	124
Can You Hear Me Tap – *Tammy Nuzzo-Morgan*	125
Ode to an Old Woman – *Marna Broekhoff*	126
One Bare Place Setting – *Louis Hoffman*	128
Trying to Manage – *Aliya Granger*	129

The Heavens Cried – *David Bentata*	131
The Ghost in my Abdomen – *Candice Hershman*	132
Spirit – *Robert A. Neimeyer*	133
Over the Hill – *Ted Mallory*	135
Many Years Have Passed – *Laurie Phillips*	138
Armin's Shoes – *Grace Harlow Klein*	139
Death Poem #22 – *Richard Bargdill*	141
Tree People (Image) – *Richard Bargdill*	142
Survivors – *Robert A. Neimeyer*	143
Parts of Speech – *Carol Barrett*	145
Death's Courting – *Louis Hoffman*	147
The Desert of My Youth – *Larry Graber*	149
Swimming for Treasures – *Nance Reynolds*	151
The Boy They Love – *Lisa Vallejos*	153
Reptile – *Nesreen Alsoraimi*	154
Black Coffee – *Catherine Granger*	155
Hell's Gate – *Kat V. Rosemond*	156
The Weeping Tree – *Erica Palmer*	158
The Crestone Experience – *Juanita Ratner*	159
At Grandma's Feet – *Lisa Vallejos*	162
Vicissitudes – *Shelley Lynn Pizzuto*	163
Tractor Ride – *David Bilyeu*	164
Sharing Grief – *Tracy Lee Sisk, Kat V. Rosemond, & Larry Graber*	166
All I Have is Silence – *Paul T. P. Wong*	171
I'm So Sorry – *Ted Mallory*	172
Approaching Death – *Louis Hoffman*	175
In Trees Again – *Victoria J. Hamdi*	176
Choosing to Turn – *Michael Moats*	177
Road Kill – *Nesreen Alsoraimi*	180
Alter – *LeesaMaree Bleicher*	181
Unfinished Narrative – *Joy L. S. Hoffman*	183
The Cross Culture Citizen – *Eylin Margarita Blake*	184
Only Here & Only Now – *Samuel Ballou*	185
The Dam Cannot Hold – *Amelia Isabel Torres*	186
Letting Go – *Ericka Pate*	188
Thirst – *Emily Lasinsky*	189
Cloak of Happiness – *Chelsea McCarty*	191

Pushed into the Wilderness – *Monica Mansilla*	192
Room – *Robert A. Neimeyer*	193
Growing – *Molly Kruger*	195
Hollow – *Ashley Finley*	197
Surviving the Loss – *Carrie V. Pate*	199
Snowfall – *Carol Barrett*	200
I mumbled – *Anne YJ Hsu*	202
Unnamed – *Tammy Nuzzo-Morgan*	203
Alzheimer's Disease – *Erica Loberg*	204
The Lost Home – *Monica Mansilla*	206
Stanstead – *Victoria J. Hamdi*	207
Fourteen Years – *Michael Moats*	209
The Undertaking – *Beverly Magovern*	211
Again – *Lisa Vallejos*	212
Dandelion (Image) – *Richard Bargdill*	213
The Threshold – *John Chavis*	214
Sometimes – *Judith H. Montgomery*	215
Bitter Watch – *Kat V. Rosemond*	218
On Pain and Healing – *Melinda Rothouse*	221
Falling Apart – *Candice Hershman*	223
Alma – *Victoria J. Hamdi*	225
Processing – *Emily Lasinsky*	227
Blue – *Amelia Isabel Torres*	228
Horse of Snow White – *Jesse S. Moats*	229
I Stand – *Shawn Rubin*	230
Send-off – *Robert A. Neimeyer*	233
The Return of Spring – *Paul T. P. Wong*	235
Poetry Exercises	237
About the Editors	245

Acknowledgements:
A Testament to Meaning in Relationships

We would like to thank Nesreen Alsoraimi for her valuable and insightful assistance in reviewing a large number of poetry submissions, as well as being a contributor to this project with her heartfelt expressions of loss. Symbolic of the grieving process, to complete a project such as this it is necessary to have support that incorporates individuals with different strengths, perspectives, and compassionate hearts, who are willing to be present and offer themselves to the process. Nesreen's work and assistance were indicative of these and were very much appreciated.

Carol Barrett, Candice Hershman, and Richard Bargdill supported this project beyond their own contributions with encouragement and assistance in recruiting some of the wonderful poets who contributed to this volume. Thank you.

The many wonderful writers and poets who contributed their poems to this project deserve our deepest gratitude. The willingness to share one's poem when it embodies deep pain and loss is an act of courage. We appreciate the courage as well as the art of our many contributors.

We would like to thank University Professors Press for supporting this project and its openness to recognizing that this is a project that transcends genres, to at once be academic, a book of art, and a book of healing. We would especially like to thank Jim Ungvarsky and Shawn Rubin at University Professors Press for their support for this project.

From Louis...
Writing the acknowledgements of a book is always a deeply emotional experience for me. Each time I near completion of a book I find myself filled with deep gratitude. As I journey into expressing my gratitude, I am drawn to worrying that many

readers may skip over this important section. My hope is that they can share a small portion of my gratitude even if they do not know the individuals acknowledged. Writing never happens in isolation. While I believe this is always true, I know it is profoundly true for me. If you enjoy this book and you know anyone mentioned in this section, I hope you can share in the gratitude for the amazing people who helped this book become a reality.

Writing for me is a passion, but it is also a sacrifice. I do not write for a living; I write because I have accepted that it is part of who I am and I can do no other if I am to be authentic with myself. Because I do not write for a living, my family often carries the brunt of the sacrifice. I first must thank Heatherlyn Hoffman, my amazing wife, best friend, and life companion. For years I have tried to write you the perfect poem, but I have never been able to write one that comes close to matching the love I have for you and the beauty you bring to my life. I will feebly keep trying to find the words, but I know words are finite, too, and will always fail in matching my love for you. I hope you always know that part of why I must write is because you fill my life with so much that I cannot keep it hidden. Thank you for tolerating my compulsion to write, and thank you for keeping me inspired.

I want to thank my sons, too, who are still too young to understand the sacrifice. I try to keep it hidden from you, writing at night and the early morning hours so it that you will never have to feel jealous of the tapping of the keyboard when you want to cuddle or play. You have inspired so much in my life and so many of my poems. I love you Lakoda. I love you Lukaya. I love you Lyon. You keep every day filled with wonder and awe.

I want to thank my parents, Clarence and Lynn Hoffman. I dedicated this book to you not simply as a token of appreciation for being my parents, but for all that you have contributed to my life extending well beyond parental obligations. When I think of character and compassion, I have no doubt about where these values come from in my life. You have lived these and fostered their development in me. I look at your lives and I know the world is a better place because you have graced it. You have also given the gift of presence. You have been there, even when I didn't realize it or ask for it. You were there loving, caring, and holding. Without that, I would not be the man I am today.

I would like to thank Jason Dias, who is a wonderful and talented writer, but also a regular encouragement in writing. Jason's commitment to writing is inspiring and his encouragement to keep prioritizing writing is deeply meaningful. I would like to thank Willson Williams, Shawn Rubin, Steve Pritzker, Ruth Richards, Theopia Jackson, and Stanley Krippner, who are wonderful colleagues at Saybrook University and have provided meaningful encouragement in my writing. I also would like to express my deep appreciation for my brother and sister-in-law, John and Joy Hoffman, for their constant encouragement in writing and life, as well as my friends Glen Moriarty, Nathaniel Granger, Jr., Brittany Garrett-Bowser, Mark Yang, Xuefu Wang, and Dan Hocoy.

Last, I want to thank my friend and colleague, Michael Moats. Writing is sacred to me, especially when it comes to poetry. To share in a collaborative project such this is a deeply meaningful and bonding experience. As we have worked through this project, my deep respect and appreciation for the person you are—your character, integrity, and heart—has continually grown. Sharing in this project, and our friendship, is something I will always cherish.

From Michael...
As usual, my wife, Annie, has been continually supportive and encouraging of my interests and aspirations, as well as supportive of my colleagues. We have been a team through losses, trials, achievements, life transitions, and dreams, and this project was no different. To be willing to sacrifice 'our' time to be in agreement with work that is for the greater good and greater community is a wonderful blessing to have with a spouse, and this is my wife. Thank you, Annie!

My parents have been instrumental in creating a foundation of whom I am and helped to shape me along my journey. They taught me to take life as it comes and to make choices based on integrity and character. My mother has died, and the lessons she taught me in living, in dying, and in death opened my eyes to a perspective in life that would otherwise have been unseen. My dad has always been supportive through his belief in me, through the depths of symbolism, and through his gifts of wisdom, given freely and accepted humbly. I am also excited that both my dad and I have poems published in the same book. What an honor!

Louis Hoffman has, at different times, been a mentor, a colleague, and a friend, and I am proud to still call him all three. From early on in my career he has gone out of his way to create or point out opportunities for growth, to chase dreams, to gain life-changing experiences, all quietly, without expectation, and selflessly. Thank you, Louis!

Setting the Context

It is our hope that *Capturing Shadows* is experienced as more than a book of art; we hope it is a book of transformation. As you prepare to embark upon the journey of these poems, we want to invite you to engage in an activity intended to deepen your experience of this book. Take a few minutes to complete the following activity before you begin reading the rest of the book.

Before reading this book, complete the following sentences below:

I thought of loss (in any form) as:

I felt loss was:

I was:

Loss held:

Preface

This book of poems by psychotherapists and other healing individuals is long overdue. It addresses three significant facts. First, psychotherapists and other healers are humans with deep feelings struggling to make meaning of the experience of grief and loss. This fact is clear in every page from very diverse authors. It is rare in the world of psychotherapy that we encounter psychotherapists openly exploring one of the most profound and humbling human experiences: grief and loss.

Second, these diverse authors attempt to make meaning of grief and loss through the artistry of poetry. Each author uses both the simplicity and complexity of grief and loss through poetry. This fact brings into our awareness—these psychotherapists and healers are poets. These poets have the great privilege of holding and helping clients transform their pain of grief and loss. It is through their professional and personal experiences of grief and loss that we hear poetry from the heart. Their words will move and inspire you.

Finally, these poets take us with great courage into the shadows of grief and loss. They do not invite the reader to "get over it" (grief and loss) but rather invite you to explore the pain with all the shadows associated with grief and loss that can lead to transformation.

Many years ago I read an anonymous quote, which I treasure:

> Pain is the great teacher
> Never flee from it
> It bestows wisdom, courage and eternal life.

Each of us encounter pain with grief and loss. This book has the potential of becoming a much-needed mentor when encountering grief and loss. To find one book of poetry with this rich potential of transformation is truly a gift. I have volunteered for over thirty years for Hospice of Petaluma and am always referring clients and colleagues to books. I am relieved to know there is finally one book of poems I can refer individuals to for support, honesty, and compassion with grief and loss.

Myrtle Heery, PhD
Author of *Awakening to Aging*

Foreword

When someone you love dies, you naturally grieve. You experience many thoughts and feelings inside yourself. Grief is your internal struggle. It is the unavoidable, intrinsic counterpoint to love.

Mourning is when you express your grief outside yourself. Mourning is crying, talking about your loss, and participating in a support group. Mourning is also writing and creating artwork. Mourning is essential, because it is through active mourning that you move forward on the journey to healing.

Writing poetry about loss is a form of mourning. So is, I would argue, reading poetry. When you spend time with the poems in this book, you engage your inner thoughts and feelings about your loss with the thoughts and feelings of someone outside yourself. You empathize. You feel. You acknowledge and embrace your love and loss. You remember. You consider your new life. You try to find meaning in what was as well as what will be.

In this way, loss poems are like small, precious parcels of healing that you can unwrap at any time. Pick up this book, read a poem, sit with it for a moment in the shadows, then continue on with your day.

Louis Hoffman and Michael Moats are among the rare therapists who truly champion the necessity and nature of healthy grief and mourning. They have compiled this poignant collection because they understand that poetry not only speaks to mourners, it helps transform them.

Grieve, engage, mourn, and heal.
Godspeed.

Alan D. Wolfelt, PhD
Author of *Understanding Your Grief: Ten Essential Touchstones for Finding Hope and Healing Your Heart*

Introduction:
Capturing Shadows with Poetry

Good art wounds as well as delights. It must, because our defenses against the truth are wound so tightly around us. But as art chips away at our defenses, it also opens us to healing potentialities that transcend intellectual games and ego-preserving strategies. (May, 1985, p. 172)

An Invitation to the Shadows

Ah, grief, I should not treat you
like a homeless dog
who comes to the back door
for a crust, for a meatless bone
I should trust you.

I should coax you
Into the house and give you
Your own corner,
A worn mat to lie on
Your own water dish.
~ Denise Levertov (2001)

Too often we think of grief and loss—whether from death, divorce, or other life transitions—as something that we must "get through" or "get over." We do not think of the gifts of grieving. This is not to say that the loss itself is good or something we should be thankful for, but rather it is acknowledging the blessings that emerge when we trust the grieving process and sit in the darkness of grief, capturing the shadows.

This is what this book is about: Capturing the shadows of grief and loss, and allowing them to transform us. Trusting them. Treasuring them. Sharing them.

The origins of the book emerged from our own interest in poetry for healing in our personal lives and our role as psychotherapists who have walked the path of healing with so many grieving souls. Our faith in the healing potential of poetry was built through walking these paths over and over. As LuXun (1921/1961) states, "hope cannot be said to exist, nor can it be said not to exist. It is just like the roads across the earth. For actually the earth had no roads to begin with, but when many men pass one way, a road is made" (p. 191). Poetry is a well-traveled path to healing and transformation.

Trusting the Shadows

As therapists, we often witness powerful transformations that occur in the shadows as well as the fear and anxiety present when approaching them. The fear and anxiety makes sense. Henri Nouwen (1979) notes that it is difficult to go into the depths of one's pain without faith that there is something better on the other side.

This faith or hope is not an easy thing to come by. For many, poetry provides a safe medium to enter the darkness and they feel drawn to it. For others, the honesty of poetry may feel as if it is too much. Yet, poetry is one on of the oldest healing arts and has been used across many cultures long before therapy and other more contemporary forms of psychological healing emerged (Hoffman & Granger, 2015). In many ways, the healing journey of poetry has been paved by the hope of many generations across numerous cultures. If we can join in that hope, and share in the stories of those who have been touched and healed by entering the shadows, we may be able to begin finding our own healing.

Embracing the Darkness

Few artists have shown greater reverence for the darkness to be found in the shadows than Bruce Springsteen. Throughout his lyrics, darkness is one of the most pervasive themes. Springsteen does not idealize or glorify darkness, but rather gives darkness its due reverence. In the documentary *The Promise* (Landau & Zimny, 2010), the narrator illustrates that Springsteen's album *The Darkness on the Edge of Town* is a transforming moment in his legacy. Springsteen's earlier work embraced idealized dreams of running away. In these early albums the lyrics still grappled with the pain, but did not show the depth of reverence for it that later would develop.

In "Thunder Road," Springsteen sings to his lover, "So Mary climb in, it's a town full of losers and I'm pulling out of here to win." In "Born to Run," although Springsteen tells Wendy, "Together we can live with the sadness," he is painting an idealistic vision beyond it:

> Someday girl I don't know when
> We're gonna get to that place
> Where we really wanna go
> And we'll walk in the sun
> But till then tramps like us
> Baby we were born to run

But then comes *Darkness*. In *Darkness on the Edge of Town*, The Boss (i.e., Springsteen) is done running. In the title song, which embodies this shift in both energy and lyrics, Springsteen has found a home in the darkness on the edge of town. This is not a gloomy place; it is a place of transformation. It is a place, "For wanting things that can only be found in the darkness on the edge of town." The edge of town, where the shadows overtake the light, is a place of redemption; it is a place of emerging hope. The edge of town is also the place where the shadows meet the light. In *Capturing Shadows*, like

Springsteen's *Darkness on the Edge of Town*, we seek healing and transformation that can only be found when we are willing to capture and stay with the shadows.

Embracing the Pain

> ...less and less is life animated through personal discovery, intimacy with others, or self-reflection. While life has become more manageable for many people, it has become commensurately less engaged. (Schneider, 2004, p. 20)

As therapists who have specialized in working with grief, it is common for clients to come to therapy struggling with the expectations put upon them about how they are supposed to grieve. Too often, they have heard well-intentioned people offer phrases such as, "It will get better with time," "They are in a better place," and "Time heals all wounds." While these may come with good intentions, they give the grieving person the message that they should not be grieving. Yet, holding the pain in does not work; it needs to find its expression. For some, poetry becomes a safe place where they can express their pain and grief without judgment. As we learn to embrace the pain, we begin learning how to live with it.

Melting Snow was written throughout the day that I (Michael) knew I could wait no longer to put my dog down. It had been coming, but this day there was no more denying what had to be done. At different times during the day and immediately following her death I used the ink and paper to hold the strong and painful emotions as a way to release, to find courage, and to cope. It was also something that I could hold onto and read after the veterinarian took my old puppy from the home; it was a useful tool to help me grieve.

During the grieving process that can follow all types of loss there are numerous opportunities of engaging the pain and confusion of these life changes that leave one wanting, desiring. Poetry will not fill the hole of loss, but it can provide a home for the feelings and maybe even an alternative. *A Mother's Hug* was written when the greatest desire of my (Michael) heart for that day was to be able to once again feel the hug of my mother. The reality is that I will never again physically feel her embrace, but as I completed the poem another reality was revealed. It was her love that has made me the hugger that I am, and I can always feel a little bit of her hug as I hug others. The tears come to my eyes even as I write this.

As we travel the roads of life we are unable to live without wounds and scars. Whether it is a single instance or a compilation of losses and pain, reflecting over one's life and the grieving one has faced can be daunting. Engaging grief changes the person forever. In one direction or another, the grieving person will be changed: diminished in despair or painfully aware of what facilitated one's growth. *Changed Lenses* was a reflection upon the death and loss that I (Michael) have witnessed thus far. The poem is not a rainbows and unicorns poem, to say the least, and bears witness to the scars of having lived surrounded by death. Not filled with flowery words or even optimism, it is the resolute ending that succinctly holds the promise of the continued value for living alongside the pain.

The Use of Poetry

Poetry can be a useful tool to work through what is not understood and even what is not yet conscious, and helps us make meaning in our self-world relationship, as well as giving clinicians insight into the clients' experience or perspective. Pennebaker, Zech, and Rimé (2001) note that research is continuing to show the physical and emotional benefits of utilizing written word to process difficult emotions. Similar to other forms of expressive arts, poetry is a projective medium that allows one to take one's emotions, thoughts, images, perceptions, and experiences and place them at a semi-safe distance in which to process (Hoffman, Hershman, & Moats, 2011).

When we read or write a poem something happens within us. We can encounter our emotions (Near, 2012) in a deeper way that helps to facilitate the client's reconstruction of their current narrative (Neimeyer, 2001). The words on the page awaken an awareness of connection. The individual can begin to see a framework for their pain and emotion, building bridges between hidden pain, expressions of courage, clarity of understanding, and the fragmentation (Kauffman, 2002) that can accompany traumatic loss. This framework can create symbolic "containers for overwhelming emotions" (Stepakoff, 2014, p. 66). What better container to hold one's emotions than one that has been created by the individual himself?

Not everyone experiences poetry the same way. The very word "poetry" can cause people to freeze in fear and self-doubt. In *Defense of Poetry,* Shelley (1840) wrote "every author is necessarily a poet, because language itself is poetry" (as cited in Mazza, 2003). Poetry can be seen as rigidly adherent to structural beats and rhythms or something much freer and less restrictive. At times the structure helps contain the pain to keep it manageable, at other times it can be overly constraining and repressive. For some the freedom of poetry opens one up to the deeper experience and possibilities, at other times it overwhelms. There is no right or wrong, as long as it is the author's chosen form and from her or his voice. Yet, it can also be helpful to stretch oneself to play with different approaches to poetry. The anxiety felt when approaching poetry can be an invitation, not a warning. As one becomes more comfortable with different emotional experiences, new forms of poetic consumption and expression open up.

Poetry in Therapy

Psychotherapy has a long history of engaging the creative arts and even developing approaches to therapy based upon the arts, such as art therapy, dance therapy, and poetry therapy. The use of the arts is particularly common with certain types of therapy, such as existential, humanistic, Jungian, and constructivist psychotherapy. While some forms of therapy use the creative arts as a basis for therapy, others integrate the arts into established approaches to psychotherapy.

There are many ways that poetry can be utilized in the therapy process. A therapist can ask the client to bring in a poem that he or she connects with or a poem that encompasses who they are. These can build rapport by demonstrating interest and gaining insight into what the client is facing, such as loss, in a less emotionally threatening manner. A poem also can be given to a client to read or discuss. Clients are not asked to interpret the poem or identify the *true* meaning, but rather the personal meaning the poem has for the client. When the therapist initiates the use of an established piece of work, it is important to know your client's interests, what would be offensive, possible triggers, and what they are trying to face. Bowman (2012) adds an additional option of asking the client what he or she might say to the author after reading the poem.

If needed, a therapist can give their clients a sense of structure for security, or provide them the freedom and acceptance to lay it out in any form that fits with their personality. Writing poetry may originally seem like verbal vomit; however, the act can be powerful when the words are released without judgment or restriction, and then, if one choses, going back through them purposefully with the secondary lenses of rationality and creativity. It gives the client the ability to symbolically construct meaning in a purposeful manner that can translate into her or his belief in their ability to do the same in other areas of their life.

Freedom without adherence to form.

In fact, it is not about judgment of form, and form cannot be allowed to supersede the importance of content or the freedom of expression by the client. Poetry is more than just putting emotion into ink. Poetry is a relationship; a relationship of images, experiences, thoughts, emotions, language, perceptions, motion, and vulnerability. All of these are relationships. They are connections being built or reestablished following the loss of a friend, a spouse, a home, a job, or even a stage in life. Poetry is not just an expression, but rather engages life on multiple levels.

When read aloud, it further deepens the experience. There is a lot of power in hearing one's own voice. We often do not pay attention to our own voice when speaking. Yet, when voicing emotions and vulnerabilities, the power of expressing and relating to one's voice can create a different intensity of awareness. After working with a client that had grown frustrated and was having difficulty recognizing her progression, I (Michael) began reflecting on our work together and was trying to figure out a way to help her see what I had been observing. I woke up one morning at about 4 am with an idea: Poetry! ...She'll hate it... and probably love it. One thing I knew, though, was that I needed to meet her half way. I needed to give her *some* structure to meet her personality. I began typing a template for a poem with minimal input from me, but with enough structure to hold the thoughts and emotions of my client's journey. The initial part of this exercise is included prior to this introduction.

This poetic structure uses the past, present, and future, and asks questions about thoughts, feelings, self-view, and life's value within the specified timeframes. I then interject a few lines to tie it together poetically, with a final blank for the client's current purpose. It allows the client to see and consolidate her journey and pathway from the vantage point of today by capturing the past, assembling the present, and projecting the future. I explained to her that I had created a skeletal structure for a poem that had been filled in with her words from the questions I had asked during the session. I shared that there were three lines that were mine, but the rest was hers. Similar to therapy, I only provide a structure to help her engage with her thoughts, emotions, and experiences in a different way, and the few lines I added were symbolic of our therapeutic journey together in helping her live the existence she desires.

As she read it aloud, she began to cry. The pace of her reading caught my attention more than the words, somewhat rapid and painfully sharp for part and slower with more peace yet subtle fear with the other. When she was finished I asked her to let me read it back to her. I tried to mirror her pace. She began to cry a bit harder at first and then seemed to find solace and insight upon my finishing. She said that she could understand why she wanted to hurry though part of it; it was a physical and emotional reaction that she had with one word when she read it, and again when I read it, which caught her attention.

She said that even though she wrote the poem, it had not shown itself until she could also hear it by her voice and then again by mine. The work we had done previously helped her to pay attention to these twinges that she was now noticing. The word that she was triggered by was "healing," which was important because she had felt "broken." Using written as well as spoken-word poetry, we were able to deepen our relationship and create a connection that she had been missing. She was in a poetic relationship that allowed her to safely experience her pain and appreciate what she still had to offer, in spite of her loss.

Connecting Meaning

> At some point we sit alone while a loved one goes through a transition and as much as we have learned or happen to know, there is a helplessness that does not sit easy. My moment came when laying on the bed in the dark feeling helpless and listening to a storm door creaking and banging against the frame slowly in the wind. An owl outside my window, perfect. We are willing to reach to the magic, the great mystery, our faith that has worked for us in the past to please do it for us once again. It doesn't become a how to or a seven step process, this is the moment of a command or of a prayer.
> Wade Agnew (Personal Communication)

Viktor Frankl knew suffering and loss well. During World War II, he was placed in the concentration camps, not knowing whether his family was alive or dead. Many people he cared about died in the concentration camps while he was there, and he learned of the death of others after he was released. According to Frankl (1984), "suffering ceases to be suffering at the moment it finds a meaning" (p. 117). Frankl is not suggesting that the pain goes away, but rather that the experience is transformed. Indeed, quite often the pain may linger for the rest of one's life, but the intensity and experience of the pain changes in a way that is more bearable. An example of making meaning in loss came following one of the largest fires in Colorado history. A group of artists collected burnt pieces of the woods and created charcoal drawings in which they then sold at an auction and used the proceeds to help fund the reseeding of the very woods from which they collected the materials; a collective, poetic action in grieving. Eventually, new growth will surround the burnt wooden remains, a deeply symbolic picture of grieving.

One of the beauties of poetry is its availability to the soul and the experience, whether processing early anticipatory emotions, immediate anticipatory struggles, grieving after loss, or reflecting at a distance. The poem, *Let Me Help You, Dad*, was written during my (Michael) work on an in-patient hospice floor in which I observed a son caring for his father. There were parallels between this picture of love and respect that mirrored the relationship between my dad and I. Although my dad is alive and well, this encounter provoked some feelings that needed to be addressed and my processing resulted in that poem.

The poem *Let Me Be Ready* was written while I (Louis) was flying to visit my mother, who was in an induced coma. On the plane with many strangers, the tears began to flow and drip onto my iPad as I typed the words. I wanted to hide the tears from those surrounding me who would not understand, but I knew it was more important to write the poem. The poem speaks to the fear and anticipatory pain of losing my mother too soon. My mother has since recovered, but the poem preserved an important lesson for me: I am not ready. I don't know that I will ever be ready for this loss, but now I am committed to living more fully with the reality that I want to treasure every moment I can with her and my father, and that I want to make sure my sons remember the love of their grandma and the love they have for her. This poem, since her recovery, is a reminder to live, and to live more fully.

Relationships

The night my (Louis) dog, Amaya, died, the poem *I Had to Say Goodbye Tonight* began to form in my thoughts while driving home from the animal hospital. While my vision was still blurred by tears, my emotions found clarity in the poem. Once home, I cried, and sometimes sobbed, as I wrote out the poem. When it was done, something shifted. The grief was far from over; still is. I went to greet Dante, our other dog, who did not know his sister was not coming home. Even with him nuzzling my hand, the yard felt the loneliest it had ever felt.

One of the challenges with grieving a pet is that you inevitably are met with the reaction, "It is just a dog." Sometimes, this reaction is in words, but more often it is left unspoken, yet evident. I sent the poem along with the news of Amaya's death to four of my friends spread from California to China who I knew would understand my pain. As their responses came back the next day, I felt their shared tears, though I never saw them; I felt their love.

Grieving rituals serve a purpose. As they are passed on from generation to generation, it is easy to become disconnected from their purpose. When we lose someone or go through a significant life transition, these rituals help us on the path of grieving. The loss of a relationship creates a gap in our support system. Grieving rituals involve a social or relational component to them helping us rebuild our support system, and to feel the love lost through the establishment of new relationships.

I (Louis) regularly teach courses and lead workshops on poetry and healing. It is common for people in these courses and workshops to comment on the intimacy of poetry. This is part of its sacredness. It reveals us in ways that we normally do not reveal ourselves. To share one's poetry is an act of vulnerability and courage. Those who open themselves to hearing the poems recognize this; however, not everyone opens himself or herself as a listener. They may be quick to judge the aesthetics or mechanics of the poem, or set their mind to correctly interpreting the poem. This often places a barrier between the receiver of the poem and the poet, sometimes even the poem itself.

Intimate relationships require vulnerability and openness. Receiving a poem with openness is also vulnerable. It is opening oneself to being changed through connection with the poem and the very real person who wrote the poem. There is something beautiful when the receiver of a poem recognizes its sacredness and holds that with love and compassion. As I hope is evident, we are not talking about intimacy and love in a romantic sense, although this would apply to romantic relationships as well. We are speaking to the intimacy, love, and compassion that can exist between two people who may not even know each other well, but choose to open themselves to each other in a moment of vulnerability.

Holding Paradoxes

> If someone told me that I could live my life again free of depression provided I was willing to give up the gifts depression has given me—the depth of awareness, the expanded consciousness, the increased sensitivity, the awareness of limitation, the tenderness of love, the meaning of friendship, the appreciation of life, the joy of a passionate heart—I would say, 'This is a Faustian bargain! Give me my depressions. Let the darkness descend. But do not take away the gifts that depression, with the help of some unseen hand, has dredged up from the deep ocean of my soul and strewn along the shores of my life. I can endure darkness if I must; but I cannot live without these gifts. I cannot live without my soul. (Elkins, 1998, p. 188)

Many who have read this introduction may have already noticed the pervasiveness of paradox. A paradox is something that seems contradictory or incompatible; however, is nonetheless real. Often, paradoxes integrate seemingly contradictory ideas. For example, we have spoken to the paradox that engaging one's pain and grief helps one to heal.

Existential psychology advocates that paradox is a fundamental part of being human (Hoffman, 2009; Schneider, 1999). We must disagree and argue to build deeper trust. We desire to be close to others, but also need our space. We want to grow, but often resist growth. We want healing, which requires us to enter into our pain, but also want to avoid our pain. Poetry, much more than other forms of communication, helps to hold these seemingly contradictory experiences together. This is part of the healing. Often, people become trapped in their suffering because they will only allow themselves to experience one part of the paradox.

I (Louis) have read the poem *I Had to Say Goodbye Tonight* in presentations many times. Each time I read it, the tears feel fresh. I still miss Amaya. Yet, each time I read the poem, along with the tears from missing her I also feel the joy of our love and time together. The love and joy I experienced in our relationship is part of the pain of now, and the pain of now is deeply connected to the joy of then. It would be easy to just focus on the sadness of missing her. But when I step back I can still feel the joy of our love.

I hope that I never stop missing and grieving for Amaya. It is not because I enjoy the pain, but because I want to preserve the love and joy. Similar to the quote from David Elkins above, I will gladly endure the grief of loss to preserve the beauty and joy of love. When one is able to recognize the paradox of grief, it often begins to transform the experience. The grief I feel now is different than the grief the night Amaya died. It is still grief, but it no longer overpowers me the way it did when the loss was fresh.

When we speak of healing in this introduction, we are not speaking to something that we attain. We do not heal from loss by returning to a normal state in which there is no longer any pain. This idealized conception of healing is unrealistic. The focus of healing is not a restoration to a previous state, but instead represents a new construction or understanding of oneself that incorporates the suffering through which one has traveled. Healing is better understood as a process and journey that may continue through the rest of our life. As we follow the path we are no longer captured by the shadows, but rather we capture the shadows and take them with us as memories that bind the love and the loss together.

Approach to Capturing Shadows

Capturing Shadows is more than a book of art; it is a book of healing. It bears witness to the healing of the poets through their poetry, but also is intended to help others on their healing journey. We hope this book will find its way to therapy waiting rooms, hospice rooms, funeral homes, and the personal bookshelves of many who are suffering. Yet we also hope that this book will find its way to a few syllabi for courses on grieving and loss as well as courses on poetry and healing.

When we began to approach this book our first concern was that we wanted poems that were authentic and accessible. We also sought poems from a wide array of poets. Some of the authors of this book are quite accomplished and even award winning poets. For others, this is their first time publishing, and even sharing, their poetry. We also sought to include a wide variety of poetic styles ranging from haiku to narrative poems. Some of the poems rhyme, while others do not. The diversity of voices and styles is important; each can help see the grieving process from a different angle. It may be that one poem resonates deeply during one portion of the grieving process, and another resonates more deeply at a different point of the journey.

We also wanted to approach the concept of grief and loss broadly. This is not a book of death poems, though many poems do speak to this type of loss. We often experience grief and loss at life transitions, such as the loss of a job, the loss of a marriage, children transition to living away from home, the loss of a dream, or even the loss of one's innocence. It is important that we are able to grieve for the many types of loss we experience in life.

Last, we hope that this book is used not just for consumption, but also for inspiration. We hope that in reading this book you feel compelled to grab your pen or keyboard and begin writing your own poems. At the end of the book, we have a number of suggested exercises that can be done individually or with groups. Some of these activities utilize the poems from this book while others encourage you to do your own writing. We hope these activities can deepen the healing journey.

Conclusion

Whether using this book for your own healing, to deepen your understanding of the grieving process, or with the intention of using it to facilitate guiding others on the path to healing, we hope that you are as touched and inspired by the poems in this book as we have been. In putting this book together, we have read through these poems many times, often with tears flowing. We welcome these tears, and we hope you will welcome them, too.

References

Bowman, T. (2012) Poetry and bibliotherapy. In R. A. Neimeyer (Ed.), *Techniques of grief therapy: Creative practices for counseling the bereaved*, (pp. 303-305). New York, NY: Routledge.

Elkins, D. N. (1998). *Beyond religion: A personal program for building a spiritual life outside the walls of traditional religion.* Wheaton, IL: Quest Books.

Frankl, V. (1984). *Man's search for meaning* (3rd ed.). New York, NY: Touchstone.

Hoffman, L. (2009). Introduction to existential therapy in a cross-cultural context: An East-West dialogue. In L. Hoffman, M. Yang, F. J. Kaklauskas, & A. Chan (Eds.), *Existential psychology East-West* (pp. 1-67). Colorado Springs, CO: University of the Rockies Press.

Hoffman, L., & Granger, N. Jr. (2015). Introduction. In L. Hoffman & N. Granger, Jr. (Eds.), *Stay awhile: Poetic narratives on multiculturalism and diversity*. Colorado Springs, CO: University Professors Press.

Hoffman, L., Hershman, C., & Moats, M. (2012, February). *The use of poetry in psychotherapy*. Symposium presented at the 6th Annual Conference of the Society for Humanistic Psychology, Santa Barbara, CA.

Kauffman, J. (Ed.). (2002). Safety and the assumptive world: A theory of traumatic loss. In *Loss of the Assumptive World: A Theory of Traumatic Loss*, (pp. 205-211). New York, NY: Brunner-Routledge.

Landau, J. (Producer), & Zimny, T. (Director). (2010). *The promise: The making of the Darkness on the Edge of Town* [Motion Picture]. United States: Thrill Hill Productions.

Levertov, D. (2001). *Poems 1972-1982*. New York, NY: New Directions.

LuXun (1959). My old home. In Y. Xianyia & G. Yang, Ed. & Trans.), *Lu Xun: Selected works* (Vol. 1; p. 191). Beijing, China: Foreign Language Press.

May, R. (1985). *My quest for beauty*. Dallas, TX: Saybrook.

Mazza, N. (2003). *Poetry therapy: Theory and practice*. New York, NY: Brunner-Routledge.

Near, R. (2012). Intermodal expressive arts. In R. A. Neimeyer (Ed.), *Techniques of grief therapy: Creative practices for counseling the bereaved* (pp. 201-204). New York, NY: Routledge.

Neimeyer, R. A. (2001). The language of loss: Grief therapy as a process of meaning reconstruction. In R. A. Neimeyer (Ed.), *Meaning reconstruction and the experience of loss* (pp. 261-292). Washington, DC: American Psychological Association.

Nouwen, H. J. M. (1979). *The wounded healer: Ministry in contemporary society*. New York, NY: Bantam Doubleday Bell Publishing Group.

Pennebaker, J., Zech, E., & Rimé, B. (2001). Disclosing and sharing emotion: Psychological, social, and health consequences. In M. S. Stroebe, R. O. Hansson, W. Stroebe, H. Schut (Eds.), *Handbook of bereavement research: Consequences, coping, and care* (pp. 517-544). Washington, DC: American Psychological Association.

Schneider, K. J. (1999). *The paradoxical self*. Amherst, NY: Humanity Books.

Schneider, K. J. (2004). *Rediscovery of awe: Splendor, mystery, and the fluid center of life*. St. Paul, MN: Paragon House.

Stepakoff, S. (2014). Graphopoetic process. In B. E. Thompson and R. A. Neimeyer (Eds.), *Grief and the expressive arts: Practices for creating meaning*, (pp. 66-70). New York, NY: Routledge.

Poems

Opening
Robert A. Neimeyer

On the far side of your life
something calls out,
seeks union with what
it has not met.
Like the hollow of a bowl
it sculpts the shape
it must contain
in the form of its absence.
Without this fullness,
it is merely decorative,
      waiting.

Only in stillness
can you discern this void,
know the emptiness
as specific as your open mouth
or the chambers of your heart.
Only in cultivating receptiveness
like a cupped hand
can you let the world pass in
      and through,
and ready yourself
for the meeting.

The Falling of Hair
Carol Barrett

for Andrea

We sit at your bedside, handfuls
passing from brush to hand
and hand to basket, this ritual
born of the medicine that chokes
cancer. Your hair gives up
in snarled blooms stroked
from your temple, reluctant
swirls you gather and pass;
brush, gather, pass.
You feared this undoing
would take weeks. Instead
we make an evening of it, touching
the new frame of your face,
hair looped round our fingers,
insistent rings. What you give me:
a part of yourself, the fine rays
having risen and set with you
forty-odd years. I take
into my hands what petals
reveal of the world, vulnerable
patch on your scalp growing,
the fear that in the end,
there will be no new self
strong enough to walk the wind.

The basket receives its strands,
carries them away. And even
as we pat this firm new hair
in place, color-keyed
to your own, we are made ready
for Easter morning, the promise
of a new body bold in a single
stroke – that sunburst

day a handful
closer, when you will look
out from thickly rooted locks
to behold the Savior,
face to face.

Note: Originally published in *The Christian Century*. Republished with permission.

I Had to Say Goodbye Tonight
Louis Hoffman

For Amaya

That big ol' moon wasn't quite full
As I drove home tonight
A piece of it was missing

I felt I was entering a time
Like that of tonight's moon
Without the grace of such brevity
You lay on the mat
Barely able to look up
I knew of your suffering
When even the salt of my tears
Didn't draw your tongue

I knew the decision I did not want to make

In the midst of these many strangers
I felt no shame in my tears
No desire to hold back
I never hid anything from you
And now was not the time

I wasn't ready to say goodbye
As I held your face
Cupped in my hands
I stared in those blue eyes a last time
I wouldn't look away
So the face that loved you so deeply
May journey with you from that last breath
Then they were your eyes no more

Sitting with you on the floor
At times I thought I saw a breath
I knew… I knew…

My walk felt unsteady as yours a few hours before
As I walked to my truck in that peaceful night
That held no peace for me

Back home it felt so silent
Though the noise was no different
Than the night before
That relaxed phase of crying settled in
As memories bearing the grieving process
Carried you still with me
But each time I realized
There would be no more memories
A jolt set more tears free
With gasp for air as if reaching for you
You were always my comforter

So many times I heard you were just a dog
But tonight more than ever
I wanted you to know
I never believed that lie
And tonight, as I held your face
Through that last breath
I never wanted to say goodbye

Two Balloons
Michael Moats

Today, I stared at a bunch of balloons
Blue and gold, blue and gold, blue and gold
All grouped together and pressing against the ceiling.

I spotted two in the crowd
One gold and one blue
And they were special.

With a feeling of sadness and a need for privacy
I left the house full of people,
Holding my two balloons.

The breeze was warm and light.
The pines had covered everything
In their shower of pollen.

I gaze at each of the balloons.
Their faces become clearer,
My chest becomes heavy.

Quietly I speak,
"I wish you the best, and it is time to let go."
There is a brief pause before releasing my grasp.

Still wanting to help
I gently raise my hand
As if to give the balloons an unnecessary lift.

The strings glide across my palm
As they begin their ascent.
Sadness and excitement combine.

My golden balloon respectfully and slowly began,
Until the string left my hand
And then she soared.

Direct and purposeful
She cleared the light currents
To enter the turmoil and openness that would propel her.

I watch her as my blue balloon seems to linger.
My eyes switching back and forth,
Capturing as much as I can of each.

Blue boy seems to be ready to go
But not in a hurry.
There is comfort in what is familiar.

He clings close to the towering pine
That has shielded him, yet
Careful not to attach to its projecting branches.

Almost as if he is looking around
And testing the winds for direction,
He clears the shroud of protection and goes.

A golden shimmer is almost invisible,
Invisible in the vast blue sky.
Yet, she continues to rise.

Seconds pass,
And I am left alone
With my symbolism.

Silent, sad, smiling, excited.
Reflections and dreams.
Be well, my kids.

September 11
David N. Elkins

Those planes, those buildings, those fireballs,
Those people jumping, that thick dust rolling,
Those crashing towers, those people inside,
Those firefighters, those families watching in terror
  at home, knowing their husband, wife, father, mother,
  or friend was inside those buildings, on those planes.
The Pentagon, the black scar where the plane hit,
The ones inside who never had a chance.
That Pennsylvania farm. "Let's roll," he said,
  and they did – right into eternity -- and into our hearts.
Images -- forever cut into the soul and history of America.

And then came the politics.
Americans – and allies around the world – divided, polarized.
French fries or freedom fries, take your pick and show your
patriotism – or maybe just your ideology.
Shock and Awe – and we watch it on TV.
Popcorn, anyone?
Blood on the popcorn? Don't worry. We've hired a PR firm to
  wipe it all away.
What? No weapons of mass destruction? But I thought…
Flawed intelligence or cynical politics – our nation divided,
  still torn in two, even to this day – about that day.

Sandy was 18 and Jim was 20 – and in the National Guard.
The wedding was already planned but Jim said,
"Wait until I'm home for good. I don't want to be separated
  after we're married."
He made it through three tours of duty but in his fourth the
  wedding plans,
  along with Jim's Hummer, exploded
  and Sandy and Jim's dreams broke into pieces and
  flew 2,000 feet into the Iraqi sky.
Two weeks later, Sandy bought a one-way

ticket – some called it an overdose – to go see Jim.

But maybe today, maybe today, more than a decade later,
  maybe today we can remember:
How we came together.
How we spoke to neighbors.
How we filed onto sidewalks, into city streets and parks.
How we shook hands, or gave strangers – who somehow were
  not strangers -- a hug.
How our souls became one giant Soul
How we were one people. How *E Pluribus Unum* jumped off
  our coins and into our hearts.
Black and White, Latino and Asian, Christian and Jew, Hindu
  and Muslim,
Straight and gay, republican and democrat.
A melting pot -- a true melting pot. And we had only one name:
Americans
-- Or better yet: human beings.

And remember how friends around the world -- people in
  other countries -- sent faxes and e-mails by the millions
  saying,
"We are so sorry. So sorry -- and we are thinking of you,
  praying for you, Americans."
No longer were we "ugly Americans." The truth came out:
They were our friends – there for us when the chips were
  down.

But perhaps the thing that tore our hearts out were those
  lost people, wandering aimlessly in the aftermath, at the edge
  of the ruins, looking for any sign of their loved one.
And those notes on the fences, fluttering in the New York
      breeze, saying things like:
"Bill Johnson, if you read this, please call your family."
"Maria   Gomez. If you know where she is, call me at 555-8843
– I'm her mother."
And "Here's a picture of Daddy and me last Xmas. If you see
  him somewhere, maybe in the hospital, tell him Tammy loves

him and really, really needs to see him."

And then those readings of the names. Hours just reading names.
Names of husbands, wives, children, brothers, sisters, uncles, aunts, cousins, grandmothers,
grandfathers, friends, firefighters, policemen, flight attendants, pilots, passengers.
Would they ever stop reading those names?
Would the list ever end?
Would the pain spreading out like ripples on a lake to immediate families, extended families, close friends, other friends, business friends, church friends, temple friends, mosque friends …
Would the pain and the ripples and the names ever stop?
Would the ponds and lakes, the seas and oceans, ever be calm again?
Those names, Those beautiful names, Those beautiful, haunting names.

So here we are, more than a decade later. Remembering.
Trying to say something -- anything -- that might pay tribute, honor, to those who
Just wanted to drink their morning coffee,
Just wanted to check their overnight e-mails
Just wanted to call home to remind their husband to go to the cleaners,
Just wanted to say hi to their kids because they had left for work that morning while they were still in bed.
Yes, here we are. More than a decade later – with no words that even come close.

When Aldous Huxley was near the end of his life, the great philosopher said that it was a bit embarrassing that he had spent his entire life working on the human problem and that he had nothing of substance to offer but this:
"Try to be a little kinder."

Perhaps Aldous had it right.
We did it on "9-11". Perhaps we can do it again.
And maybe that would be the best memorial of all:
"Try to be a little kinder. Just ---"Try to be a little kinder."

Stupid Raven
Ted Mallory

I know that my Redeemer lives
Be that as it may,
There's still this
Irritating
Black bird
Rapping on my chamber door
Incessantly reminding me
Of my loss

Grief is like an earthquake
At least mine has been
I knew it was likely to come
I thought I'd prepared
Yet when it arrived I was still
Shocked & overwhelmed

What's worse,
Are the aftershocks
Never knowing when they'll come
Or how frequently
Or how hard each will be
Or how long they'll each last

I know you're better off
And in our Savior's arms
But you're not in my arms anymore
And I'm not in yours

I'm supposed to be on your shoulders
In the sun
Or slung over your shoulder
Asleep, too tired& too young
Depending on your stamina and strength land patience

But this fucking raven keeps visiting me
In my chamber
"No more, never more!"
Shut up

Stupid bird
Stupid melancholy
Stupid pain

Let me go

Rain, rain, go away
Comeback again some other day
Maybe someday when it's easier to ignore you,
Work through you
See past you

Today, you're all I know

Losing My Mind
Nesreen Alsoraimi

I'm losing my mind
Trying to distract
Myself
Losing my mind
Trying to fill this gap you left
Losing my mind
My heart's cold and it's dry
I'm trying to release this pent up energy
I feel
Closer to insanity than ever before
Closer to creativity than before
Closer to my grave
Closer to a depraved
Sense of logic
You know
I can't enjoy life like I used to
I've lost that control
I'm slipping deeper and farther
Never cried so effortlessly
Now the thought of you leaves me in a pool
Of my own sorrow
I know time is supposed to erode
This compression
This muted depression
But I tried this before
And I can't regenerate
Can't fill that space
That you made sure no one else could fit into
And I have to admit
That I love you despite it
But I hate you
For not being strong enough
To overcome it
It's sad

I'm sad
Beyond what I can handle
I overestimate my skills
I love you
I hate you
For lying
Not trying
For proving me right
Shooting me down
Every flight
Every attempt
To escape this cynicism and gloom
For giving me hope that this doom
would not be ours

Moonless Night
Juanita Ratner

The boat drifts at sea in a moonless night.
Clouds obscure the stars we would
 take our bearings from
Only an inner sense
Reaches out for the calm
Between the surges of waves
The storm
Must have blown us way off course
And yet
If our provisions only last
By the grace of God
We will drift
Until some signs enable us to divine
What course we may prevail....

Our destination?
Now unknown
The goal we sought
May not even exist
As in the days of old
When new lands were discovered
By those explorers who set out simply
To find a new way
To a land they thought was there

What strange course
Lord
You prompt your explorers to discover

As we breathe to find a pathway
Through the iron tenseness of anxiety and doubt
When our minds scramble and clutch
As if to grab some magic formula
Even surrender seems a trick

Mocking thoughts could tear the heart asunder

And even bad poetry seems somehow
In its very humility
The only peace.

Passage of Sorrow
Nance Reynolds

A wintry January night, a dreariness draping every scene
Rain pounding on rooftops- holding a spirit of defiance.
Stopping in the chapel for some reason, on my way...

We watched her walk in around midnight.
Full belly. relaxed stride. "maybe 3 centimeters" we say- "or 4"
A long way to go... we nod.
Musing as we did, a story or some laughter,
Idiosyncrasies shared,
to find comfort and communion til dawn.
Creating our corner in the nightscape of the hospital,

In a few hours there was a bustle- never welcome.
And then a prophetic silence...
The next night, the weeping mother was under my watch,
To be with, to join- in some small way with the pain and loss,
 To attempt comfort.
When there is none in this whole world.

Rain pounding still, windows cloaked in sheets of wet.
Through heaving sobs and animal noises of grief.
The weeping woman shared many stories,
    words woven with yearning, anticipation, shock,
    and then descent...into darkness.
We both touched the baby's new clothes with gentle reverence..
Listening, opening, allowing, offering...
Yet no relief,
Grief, the force of all forces.

On the third night – entering the room, there was silence.
Silence and soft echoes of ivory petals fallen to the floor.
 Exhaustion without interruption.

Touching the weeping woman's shoulder,
Only to let her know I was there with her,
... our eyes met.
And there was a new moment.

Just barely, beyond the circle of exhaustion and numbness.
was an infinitesimally tiny presence
    as quiet as breath itself,
Right there, the wheel of grief moved toward….

Atonal Autumn
Candice Hershman

Atonement in tones,
autumn
where we see dead things
despite fresh grass born
beneath our feet.

This is an entire season
captured in slow motion,
breathing in and out,
all of these voices opening
like flowers,
harnessing chaos
in trembling air and mouths
that come so close to the garden
by way of sound,
and sound is a road:
a dimensional road
full of binding sentiments
bidding reminders
of lichens and post rain moss,
yellow leaves and fallen pods
that feel like cat's ears,
muddy paths
and blustery air enlivening,
fallen branches showing
that there are seasons
within the season,
that decay is so alive,
that we take fungus for granted.

I want to hear it,
the un-orchestrated song
of a man who knows
warm colors in cool air

the way my favorite poet
understood snow.

I stand in nature,
simplify myself for my own nature
and listen to sounds
that I suspect are mirrors
of my insides,
and my insides vibrate when I listen,
being played by this last phase
of Earth:
the harmonic prayer of man.
I am at the height of love,
with no need,
not even for another.
I atone with my appreciation
as all living things in Autumn
atone with a gorgeous exit.
Gratitude is the password,
uttered by presence,
heard by the everything
of what is on its way
to nothing.
As soon as I recognize beauty,
I am forgiven.

Watching Ants
Tammy Nuzzo-Morgan

At first I wanted the whole world to burn, every creature in it.
Nothing left; no sea or poem.

I didn't care about the boy next door kicking dead dandelion
   heads off his lawn,
or the bamboo shoot poking up through the tar road to get to
   sunlight.
or the ants toiling to get dirt out of their hill.
I just wanted it all to be gone, never to return.
How dare children laugh in the waves, and mothers smile in
   delight?
How dare cars stay in their lanes doing speed limits?

I wanted to sink to Hades, taking everyone with me.
No more breeze or starlight, or linguine with white clam sauce,
or two tea bags in a cup.

Then after time smoothed the jagged edges of my pain I saw
   life,
in her perpetual way, continued. She did not have the luxury of
lying in bed day and night, not caring, not wanting.

Now I stop to watch ants build, thinking how silly we all are.
But the work must continue, doesn't it?

Ode to Joseph
Lisa Vallejos

There was a gaping hole in the room when I came in
An empty space
Where your crib
Had been.

There was blood on the floor
Small, wet droplets that some
Harried nurse
Had missed.

The doctors tried to save you
Their valiant effort
To bring back life
Had failed.

I never knew you
Only your name
My memory the only proof that you
Had lived.

No Milk
Louis Hoffman

I have no milk
My son
to dry your dampened cheek
I know my touch
is not the comfort you desire
I bring you from your crib
holding you tight
you struggle and push away
to that empty spot
now cold where once lay warm
soft comforts of Mama's arms

I have no milk
My son
the bottle's not what you seek
though my love never shied away
when tears freely flowed
I always knew it was not me
to which you'd reach

I have no milk
my son
as I, too, do crave
comfort that once warmed my bed
I can no more tell
tears for me from tears for you
as our lungs take turns
grasping for air
yet as desperately as I search
still....

I have no milk
My son.

After My Death
Carol Barrett

I will wait in these poems. – Muriel Rukeyser

We never moved as one.
Our love was not meant to
flow. It bounced. We played
hardest on a long line.
Time does not tire easily.

After my death, know that I speak.
You enter a current: your knees bend
to the pull of my voice
until the wind
takes your favorite hat.
Friends will come
like thoughts.

I will love you
when it is necessary
for one of us. After my death
trust whoever will argue
and not apologize,
whoever turns from you,
returning. The tide goes out
with the moon's consent.

One wave can wash
our names from the sand.
But in these lines
a shore is forming.

Note: Originally published in *Kansas Quarterly*. Copyright held by author.

Alchemy
Wade Agnew

All the
 malfunctioned
storm door
 Does
Is
 Creek
in the breeze
 at the back
of the apartment
 an hour
and fifteen
 minutes
away
 from
an intercom
  in front of
the locked
 neuroscience
double doors
 where
the nurse
 said dryly
step back
 as you stepped
up to glance
 at the
paintings
 that line
the hall,
  but little
does the nurse
 know,
three nights
 ago

an owl
　 arrived
outside
　my window
where
　 I gave
it orders
　　to fly,
and be
 with you.

Changed Lenses
Michael Moats

Oh, how my lenses have changed.
Once shiny and new with expectations of grandeur
The world was full of curious bliss.
Intrigue, compassion, choices, unexpected storms, a calling, and examples of love,
All shaped the path of life I have explored.

Getting the call that my young niece had died,
Too surreal to fully comprehend.
Her brother's death a few years later, left only reality,
the harsh companion that would never leave again.

People would come, people would go.
Pets would die, and friendships would end.
Moves across the country and to the next block.
Jadedness and bitterness were sometimes my only friends,
But they too would go.

Breathing in and breathing out.
Some say that we live and die with each breath.
Each crashing wave, my breath was taken.
In between, reprieve and sun.

Swimming along, the waves continued.
Some by surprise, some that I challenged.
As long as I swim, there will be waves.
A reality of my present.
A strength earned from my past.

Seeing the terror in my mother's eyes
As her weakened body would only allow her hands to shake,
Flowing bile filled her mouth, stealing all breath,
Leaving her only panicked hope and voiceless cries.

Bearing witness to the countless stories of soldiers who talked with their comrades only seconds before they fell lifeless,
Just as abruptly as the whistling of the bullet that flew by.
And seeing their friends burning alive,
The screams and smells still fresh in their minds today.

Driving home to hold my wife after a long day of work
I see the lifeless body that hangs from the truck window,
I imagine he had a similar plan,
Yet his wife would only receive a phone call soon.

Stories too numerous to count
Yet each one so vivid today.
Why risk? Why try?
What is life asking of me today?

Obscured vision from the pitted windshield of my soul
Sands of lived experiences pass by with collaborated impact.
No longer can I drive idly past to view the beauty without.
It now demands my attention and requires that I pause for the relationship.

Oh how my lenses have changed.
Once shiny and new with expectations of grandeur,
The world was full of curious bliss
Curiosity, wonder, and awe still remain,
Held gently within the scarred, pumping center of my being.
The pain has been immense.

Would I do it all again, knowing the cost, knowing the heartache?
A tear on my cheek,
A knot in my stomach,
A heaviness of breath,
A faint smile that can be seen within my eyes... Yes.

The Art of Longing
Robert A. Neimeyer

This poem arose from a conjunction of events—the recent death of my mother-in-law, the last surviving parent on either side of our family, and my driving for hours through a deep Canadian winter to offer a grief workshop in Brockville. The periodic bursts of long "O" sounds echoed for me the howling wind, and the endlessly receding landscape evoked the landscape of memory and our yearning for return. The sensory pull between the strong draw of the past and my forward momentum found expression in the evolving imagery, and hinted at an essential tension in grieving.

Those of us who have driven
the long cold road alone
have watched the thin line
of trees, frosted white,
slipping behind

like memories.
We know the pull
of something unseen
beyond the reach of dry eyes,
fixed, blinking

at the distant mist.
We ride the road
with our lonely ghosts,
unwavering in their devotion
like penitents at the altar

of our grief.
This is how we perfect
the art of longing,
learn to nurse the hurt,
refuse the fullness

of this world.
For now, we keep driving,
lean into the dimming light,
lean further toward
winter's receding horizon,

and away from arrival.

The Honeymoon is Over
David Bentata

I saw the Old Man again
Many years had passed
He was alone, without his wife
So I went up close and asked

"Fifty-three years we were together
Just she & I...., we had no son
She was my moon on my dark nights
And till her death, I was her Sun"

"She helped me set up shop together
She helped when it closed down
We sold the car and then the house
While on the dole she did not frown"

"The years dragged on & some were great
But childless was our lot
We once had a false alarm
And she rushed to buy a cot"

"One day she fell into a coma
The life we'd shared was at an end
I sat by her bedside day and night
My last respects for wife and friend"

"She smiled and looked at me
And spoke these words before her final dawn
"The honeymoon is over now"
And with a sigh, her soul away was borne"

The Day the Wild Horses
Susan Gabrielle

The day the wild horses
ran down through the meadow
was the same day the rains started, signaling

the end

of the long days of solstice sleeping
which had held us captive--
fish trapped under icy rivers until thaw

You watched them from the window
slip and buck and bite
manes matted with grassy muck

Lingering in bed
I huddled beneath the white down comforter
listening to the pounding drops on the tin roof
not wanting to feel the cold splinter-filled floor boards
against my feet

Look those two are coupling, you called from the window
They must feel such freedom

When I finally joined you there
you did not take my hand

instead we watched them in silence
hitching unhitching
hitching again

The Love of a Childless Mother
Veronica Lac

"You don't know what real love is until you have
a child of your own", she says
as if the love that I feel for those in my life
is inferior to hers for her child.
Not enough to feel less than a woman,
betrayed by my body,
but now even my love is less than?
No, I will not accept that.
A childless woman I may be, but a mother I still am

No, I did not carry my child in my womb
but I hold them in my heart, always
No, I did not endure the pain of labor
but I will protect them with my life
No, I did not suffer sleepless nights
but I hold them in my arms
as they gaze at me with innocent eyes
cherishing each moment, each breath, each sigh.

My children feel the pain of separation
as much as yours,
My children thrive on my love and attention
as much as yours
My children are taught boundaries,
are disciplined when needed
and loved always.
What makes your love more real than mine?

Though mine are not human,
they are sentient souls
with their own unique ways of being in the world
and posses the talent of rendering me transparent
to the core of my being
asking only for authentic meetings

enlivening me, challenging me
to be fully present in relationships,
so that I can be courageous with you
and ask you not to dismiss my love.
For the love of a childless mother
is equally fierce, and
is equally real, and
is worth much more than you'd ever know.

A Mother's Hug
Michael Moats

A hug by no other
can match the hug of a mother.

They come when we want them
and sometimes when we do not,
but how we long for one
when they are no longer to be had.

A mother's hug is felt
to the depths of one's soul.

Her fierce love
penetrates the hardest of emotions
and provides a sense of peace,
as if the weight of the world has fallen away.

The warmth of her embrace
sows seeds of comfort
that bears fruit
in the droughts of life.

It is the life-giving connection
that is never lost
as long as you continue
to plant the warmth of this gift into others.

Your mother's vine may have dried, withered,
and have been lost to the winds of life,
but you will remain connected
through the life that you live
and the love that you give.

I Want to be Ready
Louis Hoffman

For my mother

Mama, hold on
I want to be ready
For that day
For your dark embrace
To that comforting place
Far away from the pain of now
We've come far
But are not there yet
There are words
Still hidden
Memories unborn
Grandsons, too, needing memories
More than pictures

Mama, grant me
This one selfish desire
That you alone
Would bear the pain
Let me be ready...
Suffer this for me
And when you reach your solace
Beg for my forgiveness
For this merciless wish

Written on a Plane on the Inside Jacket of a Paperback on the Way Home
Ted Mallory

no words

no images

nothing
 works well enough
there's not even
 much comfort
 in the familiar
cold comfort
 when there is

heaviness

ache

 sleep is
  no escape
when what little sleep
   actually comes

better to just
 keep moving
  slowly,
   achingly
trudging on

what else is there to do?
what else is there?
what else?
what?

A Happy Old Man
Paul T. P. Wong

He walks slowly, lest he falls.
Dim with age, he can only vaguely see,
As the world passes him by.

With a shake of head and sadness in his eyes,
He lets them strut their stuff on big stage,
And fight each other to death for a paper crown.

They compete, they fight and they die,
Learn nothing from their bloody past.

But he seems happy in his inner sanctuary,
Having no quarrel with any passer by.

Instructions For A Long Life
Carol Barrett

Read more faces, more
tombstones, more poems.
Among the sheep
and the shamrock search out
the old women.
Touch the squares of their quilts,
the blue stitches on their white
nights. Feed their cats
fish. Spare nothing.
In the morning incant the wind
to clear leaves from the gutters.
Lift the oars of their mid-day boats
and watch the evening
lie down on the lake.
Say good-bye to each day
as if it were the first.

Note: Originally published in *Touchstone* magazine. Copyright held by author.

Blessed or Cursed
Nesreen Alsoraimi

Blessed or cursed
Better or worse
I feel a wave of change
So heavy it hurts
My head is immersed
I search every corner
My truth is in there
Sometimes laying with yours
But lately opposed
Synchronized one moment
The next you're a ghost
Haunting me
Doling out a penalty
Seeping in
Blurring lines of reality
And I take the bait
Like I'm starving for another great
Travesty
Call it a fluke
But the moon is on full blast
I can feel present and past
These beams don't dance or sparkle, like day
They travel slow and shine dull on my face
On my face
There is depth in this emptiness
Steps of experience
Pulling me down
Pulling me down
Take me out of this race
Checks and balances dissipate
All worries disintegrate
Disintegrate
Out of this race
Out of this place

with you
In that space
with you

13
LeesaMaree Bleicher

we were stars
in the back seats of cars

we inhaled coke
through little pink straws
like we sipped lemonade
with all the innocence that comes with that

we stole clothes
to tease boys
white tight   tank tops
that
barely covered
our breasts

we ripped off sparkly lip-gloss
to reflect the potential we hid
instead   we used
our budding untamed sexuality
dangled it   like the cherry bomb
hidden between our thighs
feigning sighs of sweetness
to crowds of panting boys
who vied for our affections

they
gave us candy, cocaine, pills
and promises
already b r o k e n
we stood on bended knees
we learned this from the screams we heard from our parents
bedrooms late at night
when the last glass still half full

came
crashing to the floor
then our Mothers boyfriend
crept
though the bedroom door
he
came ever slower
when we cried
he
smashed ever harder
if we tried

there were no skirts   short enough
to hide the scars we wore like
the boys whose initials

we carved into the spaces our hearts were
if we grew up to be

in

Sunday school instead of detention
prom queens instead of prostitutes
valentines instead of delinquent
if we would have spent
sweet sixteen sober

if   we had it   to do all over again

Blanched
Aarica Geitner

Walls, which only prop a shell, losing sight to no avail

Tempered pressure mounting on an empty soul, Blanched, from loss of control

Eyes wide shut, unable to speak, few understand such weakness crippling to the knees

Faux expressions come easily life has taught, with veils of light your center has not forgot

Now surrender is the only thing left to face, yet recoil is what is known best to ease the pain

While shadows follow with tracks of broken hearts, time pulls you together before it lets you fall back apart

Morning will dawn new light on this life, stay connected, don't give up the fight...

Death Poem #13
Richard Bargdill

It was sad
that we had to meet
only at these events
       but nothing minor seemed
to draw us near.
His tick showed
       his apprehension.
Someone unexpected
       sent flowers.
She wanted
that trinket ,
it pissed off
the whole family.
He was a poet
       at least for today...
I wonder
if my son
will notice
       the wild horses
beyond
the graves.

A life time of rituals
for a day of reward
Even things repeated in rote
can be touching now.
Who
did
 I
cry
for?

Forever/Now
Joel Federman

I have it on my highest authority
that there are personalities
in the before-during-after-life of the psyche,
which is larger than ego,
broader than body.

Eternal life does occur.
Whether its form is satisfactory
as a balm against fear of death
depends upon the form of life we live.
If we live our lives close to the spirit
and know its heights and depths,
if we can embrace that way of being,
then we will be delighted to know
that this is the form that eternity takes,
after the motions of human being are through.

Reality is the best of cosmologies:
Personality is preserved
only in its highest dimensions.
If we do not order our lives
in accordance with the greatest realization
of the highest dimensions of our personalities,
if the whole of our personalities are dead to the eternal,
then eternity will be the death of us
as we know ourselves.

If we look beyond
the psyche of simple sight,
reaching within for the universe throughout,
then we will never fear
the forever
that is ever becoming
now.

Take my Hand...
Deerheart

The moment she touched me;
My breath escaped,
with out a sound —

Words shattered   within our dance;
She smiled a glance—

as her voice broke away,
in this moment   we knew no more —

"My love be still," as my heart filled;

A tear dropped;

We were no more —

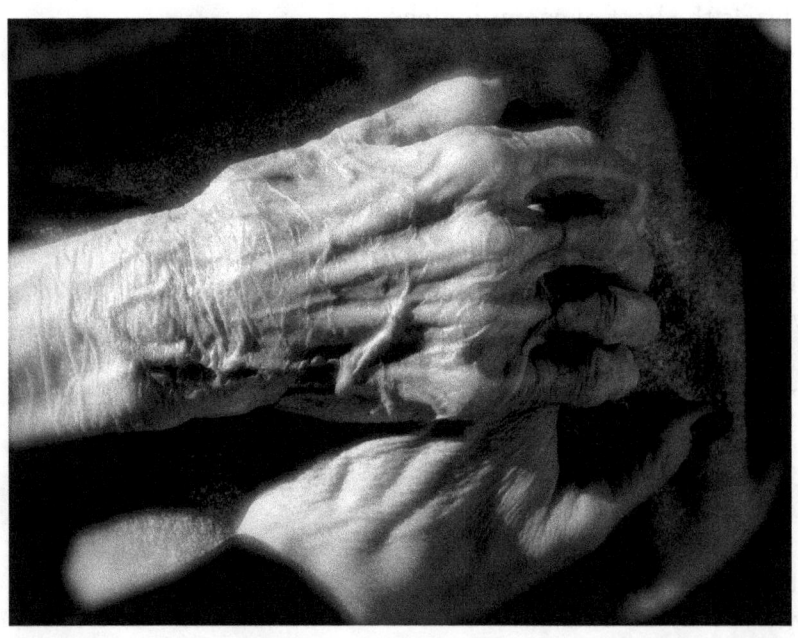

Breakfast at the Retreat
Robert A. Neimeyer

*To the survivors of Victims to Victory, and their quest to find grace
beyond the homicide bereavement that is their common bond*

The clean round tables gather the women
like open palms, call them together
for the morning meal.
Night's grasp still holds them
in silence, like the still-fresh graves
that hold their husbands, their babies,
their lives.

To strengthen themselves
to tell the story again,
suture the wounds in group,
they take their plates,
find their place,
feel the always-empty chair
for each seat filled.

A woman with moist eyes
and a blue tattoo of her daughter
on her forearm lifts the white jar,
pours sugar on her grits, forks in
the scrambled egg.

It's a Black thing, her Aunt Ethel explains,
*a way to have something sweet
when your life is poor.*

Desert Dreams
Nesreen Alsoraimi

Stepping far and fast
Too soon for past lives to take effect
Many moons and
Sand dunes made of trash
I look at days that passed and laugh at
How young
And how brash
My words and my laugh
How they didn't burn because of who you were
How we understood each other when we flew
How my hands had minds of their own
Taking turns and burning holes through
Twine and sculpture
Thick metal lights
Landing in my palms
Rushing in the night air
Wind whipping my hair
I became unstuck
attributing good fortune to luck
Those invincible nights
Those convincible nights
Flight to perplexed lands
Unbrushed strands flying by
A deck of time
fanned out and picked through
Wasted on repeated songs
And waiting too long
For a point to come across
A seahorse lost
In a vacant desert
Separating off from on
the right from wrong
Grains congregating in a flurry of
Confusion

Had I not been used to it
I would have
Been buried alive
Instead I was disillusioned
slow to step
I inched my way forward
Trading artificial light
For the shade that's slightly brighter than the darkest days
I found my way
Somehow
Without them
Without you
Without love
With only these kid gloves
and the straps on these imaginary
boots that I dare not let go of

Do You Have A Minute?
David Bentata

Hello G-d, do you have a minute?
So many questions to ask
About this world in which you placed me
After eating from that fateful tree.....
Despite the lateness....what was my task?

What was I here to do?
Have I been here before?
Where will I be tomorrow?
All I see is much pain and sorrow....
So much need and hunger.... so much war

Three score and ten we have extended
With modern medication
We live some extra years
But seldom free from worry, free from fears
So focused on the physical, while we suffer spiritual castration

And then we die, and it's all over!
Is it worth our many trips?
Or is it up to us, one and all
To learn your silent lesson, to heed your call
But no, instead we live a life of comic strips

And while we are here
We reject all our commonalities
Looking for what differences we can discern
Instead of harvesting each good action, each good turn
Ignorance and hatred reduces us to mortal casualties

G-d? ...G-d? ...Are you there?
Do not turn your back, do not despair
I know we tried to disprove your existence
Relying on science and philosophy you to outdistance
And so be free to party in our personal Vanity Fair

Teach us, for we are all your children
And all our passions and desires
We are meant to dominate
Not to them capitulate
For they'll end us all in burning fires

Your tests of Life are far too hard
Or is it that we have realised.....despite whatever we declare
That by denying your reality
It makes us free, all desires to indulge in our animal brutality
Having lost faith in our every prayer

Oh, is the minute over? ..... So fast?
I used to think my years stretched forever
But that was in my energetic youth
When I thought I was so clever

Today, full of fear, your gift of Life expended
Ignorance and doubts are now my uninvited companions
Now I see my time with you ....has just ended.

Vicious Cycle
Joy L. S. Hoffman

The best decision you ever made
Was choosing to live your own life
Embracing freedom

Freedom from guilt
Escape from judgment
Liberty from abuse

But they still have a hold
On your Heart,
Mind,
And Soul

Words deliver pain
Absence creates longing
That you don't quite understand
And you run to the
Guilt.
Judgment.
And abuse.
Because it is all you know

And you Cry.
Scream.
Blame.
Hurt.
Retreat.
And then run back for more.

And you lose a little
Of your Heart,
Mind,
And Soul

Because the loss is a down payment
For love, belonging, and connection.

It is all you know.

I fear you will never heal
Because they will not let you.
As soon as you feel whole,
They chip away
At your Heart,
Mind,
And Soul.

Because it is all they know.

Understanding Life in Death
Emily Lasinsky

Life and death,
so different in sense,
puzzles so similarly connected.
Valued dearly, but yet so dense,
not one has perfected.

Without life, how could we perish?
Crossing the finish line must first begin with one step.
Every breath of gold, cherished,
until the last breath, in the mouth is kept.

One moment existing,
the next second...
leaving others reminiscing.
Is death the black crow as we all assume,
Or is it the white dove,
a resurrection that invisibly blooms?

Some things are difficult to comprehend,
the meaning of life is one,
Our lives are spent envisioning the end,
blurry eyes until it is done.

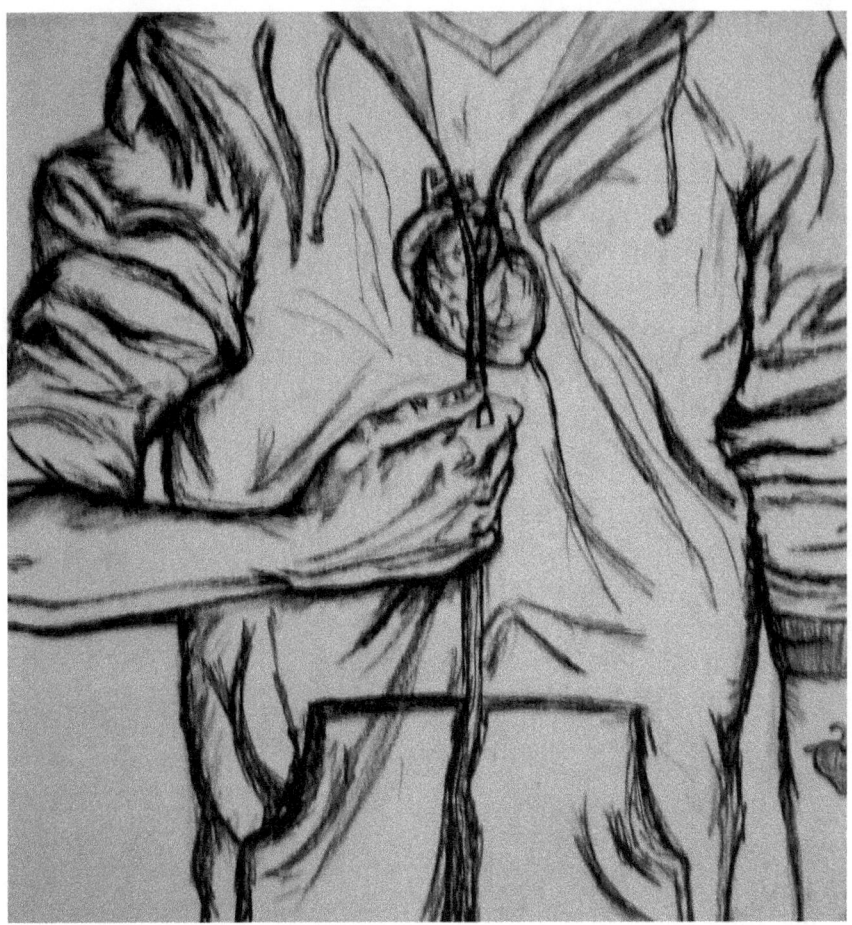

Heal by Emily Lasinsky

Brown Chair
Louis Hoffman

for my father

Smooth leather
Buttoned down and
Curved in all the wrong places
That old brown chair
Stayed at my bedroom desk
Rarely used for homework
Or drawing

Yet each night
If the fear came upon me
I would timidly come into your room
And beckon you to allay the fears
You sat patiently
Occupying that lonely brown chair
That was not built for comfort
If you got up before
My eyes stayed closed
I called out
And you stayed

Each night

You stayed

Such a seemingly simple
Act of love
Staying
Being present
Yet not til my own young son
Timidly came to my bedside
"Papa"
Did I recognize this sacrifice
This act of love

Frustrated and awakened
I remember being held in your love
And I say
"I'm right here, you are safe now."

And I know
Your love has become
My love

Little Ones
Alexandra O'Toole

Where are the little ones?
The children we held?
The smallest and best of us,
we loved them so well.
They are here! They are here,
skirting the breeze,
bringing the light, rustling the leaves.
See how their faces make everything bloom,
how their beautiful voices give rise to the moon
and the sun in its turn, the long, precious days,
the wind when it's whistling and the soft, quiet way
the dusk filters in. These are the signs,
this is the language they use. Hush now
and listen. They are here, they are here.

My Grandpa's Farm
Ted Mallory

Feels like Michigan again-
cool, damp, dewy, grassy

She'll miss her birds
She'll miss her garden
She'll miss the things the rest of us have all forgotten

She misses his touch in the middle of the night
his voice and his warmth

She's missed the children
Bright Sunday reunions

More than this,
I am afraid of missing her

Feels like Michigan
baby snow peas
baby sweet corn
dusty garages
black cherries

Feels like Michigan again

Let Me Help You, Dad
Michael Moats

I don't want to be a burden,
Says a father to a son.
My job is to care for and comfort you
Even though you are grown.

I may be lying in this bed
Unable to care for my self,
But my desire to be seen as strong
Does not fade.

Dad, it is *your* strength that you now see in me
Because you gave so unselfishly.
You taught me through your actions,
Instead of speaking empty words.

Your strength is no longer measured by your physique,
Nor is it measured by your ability to do.
Your strength is in showing me how to live
And showing me how to die.

Let me help you now, Dad.
Fore, this is what you trained me to be,
A leader through giving,
Not just another taker from the streets.

Let me help you today
And whatever days are left
Because I have no other way
To express the depth of my love.

Let me help you dad
As the man you taught me to be
So that I may pass these gifts to my children,
The lessons you are still teaching me.

Your eyes grow weary,
And your breath is weak.
Your frailty displays
What is yet waiting for me.

It seems we both are stuck
somewhere between man and child.
Living today and longing for the past,
We are faced with what is.

I am now raising my kids
And teaching them to grow,
Yet I yearn for the days where I could run into your arms
And let you make everything okay.

You gave me life
and sacrificed much of yours,
And now you are unable to raise a glass
Or to stand on your own.

Let me help you, Dad.
Let me honor you through my love.
Such a small token to give
For the life you have given me.

One Last Tear
Nathaniel Granger, Jr.

Like yesterday decades ago
I buried your body
But not the love
I'm still angry though
And, I still ask, "Why?"

They said that I would get over it
They said you were in a better place
They said, "I know how you feel."
"I lost my dog yesterday," consoled one.
Time heals all wounds.

At times, I hear your voice
Maybe not yours
'Tis mine own voice I hear
Yours, mine, I canst not tell
Your voice gave sound to my voice
Your name made you my name.

You once said, "Nothing beats a failure but a try"
I'm trying and yet I fail
To stop wondering
How life would be, could be
Had you chosen to stay.

I write, I pause, I sob hysterically
And now I bask in the saudade of your shadow
In the reflection of my own face,
Searching for what I cannot find
Where there is no rhyme or reason.

How many times my tears have become my meat
How many times have I cried myself to sleep
Trusting to see you on the morrow

But the rabbit from the magician's hat failed to appear
After tap, after tap, and tap again from the wand of time.

Do you even care—How could you?!
I used to think it was all a lie
That you feigned your death
I convinced myself but for some insurance scheme
I once saw that shenanigan played out on TV.

I patiently waited for you to resurrect from your fictitious vault
Pleading the haunting of your apparition
To relieve my suspicion
The leading man would miss the curtain call
My Savior would succumb to a finitude past my mind's eye.

You saved me from the monsters
And read to me "The Little Engine that Could"
You even gave the sip of what would morph this boy into a man
A shot of whiskey from the flask, your personal stash
It burned too my heart but never did it put hair on my chest.

My bleeding heart bleeds your blood
And yet 'tis my pain
That I am coerced to bear
No abracadabra. No hocus-pocus!
'Tis so real, I'm disillusioned—so unfair.

I wonder if you can see yourself
In your grandchildren's eyes
They're all grown-up now
My hero, my Santa, my Tooth Fairy, I think that I did good
Being half the man I believed you to be.

I am still at heart a child
But have reached an age you knew not
Your life was short, severed in youth
I am growing up, I suppose

For it have been a score and some

And, now I can look at you in mine own eye...
Do you remember?
You used to demand of me
To look you straight in the eye—
It was proof *it* wasn't a lie

Dad, I hope you can forgive me
For taking so long to forgive you.
And I toast to you before I sip one last tear.

Kindergarten Doorway/Here and Not Here
Larry Graber

Two-part poem, in loving memory of Edythe Brezin Graber (12/23/19 - 11/12/2000) Written 12/23/14 HAPPY BIRTHDAY MOM

Kindergarten Doorway

The first day of kindergarten
My mom waits by the door
Others weren't so lucky
I take the longest walk
Of my young life

strange bodies
 and faces
Surrounded me
I peer out to them
From my seat

My own place
 In the room

We are thrown
Together
Alone
Naive
To the journey
That awaits

we speckle
The long tables
Set about us
Spread with butcher paper
And paint in plastic bottles

These will be my tribe
And here is our playground

Tho right now,
I feel a held tremble
Look gingerly
So not to stare

I have a small felt sense
That we are the same

Strangers of shared purpose
and shared kind
Afraid to smile

I look back at my
Mom in the doorsill
A moments comfort
Mixed with confusion
Slight disdain
at being left
Delivered unto
This finitude

I somehow know
There is no turning back

I am absorbed
in finger paints
Their texture fills
My little pores

I feel flow
And release

Flow
And
Release

Losing track
Of clock time

I look again
Over
My
Right
Shoulder

My mother
Has slipped away
Slid past her
doorway perch
Gone

It's my paints now
Me and my tribe
Our little bodies
Form a labyrinth
Of purity and hope

The sandbox
And jungle gym
Await us

What riches
Will we find there?

Behold

My first day of kindergarten
Is almost over
And
I made it

Here and Not Here

My earliest encounter
5 years old
My mother is here and not here
At Lanai Road Elementary

40 years later
At 44
My last encounter
My mother is here
and not here
At Kaiser ICU
Woodland Hills, CA

Our most intimate bond
My lifeline fused and severed
I am completely close
Interfused, breath upon breath,
My heartbeat her heartbeat,
Our bloodline is pure
We are in total synchrony
Time has no hold on us
We see through hearts center
Our eyes have no limits
One touch draws a line
Backwards in time
To my fetal heart
One bloodstream
One thought matrix
One body
One light
Clears away
All obstructions
We are back
to our first beginning
At my mother's
last pulse chorus
All my relationships
Combine and stand
in this moment's referent
I sense the polarity
Of life/death
No separation

My biggest union
And largest loss
Irreplaceable
And ever enduring
No separation
One rhythm
Of creation
Folds into death
And my questions
Are answered
For all time
The most intimate
Is sewn of loss
It's union
The foremost affinity
Is stitched into
the underside of my flesh
I cannot take a breath
Without feeling
Its movement
this eternal scar
Expands and contracts
Connects me
Weathered by
human Frailty
And strength

Her last breath
Shook the hospital bed
Sent a life pulse through me
Marked my future
And there I was again
As before
We were here and not here
This time forever

Go My Children
Richard Bargdill

Go my children
You know the difference
between bringing life and death.
Go on your adventures
Plant trees in foreign countries
Walk the streets of strange lands
Gawk at peculiar objects
Unseen and un-thought of
In your home town.

Go my children
Run through fields
For no reason
Watch the sun fall
Over hills.
Catch the sight of odd shapes
Disturbing sounds, smells
Of the earth after rain has
Brought out the odors.

Go my children,
On your way
Become a stowaway
On the ships of life.
Let it take you and you take it
On a wild ride through rapids
Hard rocks will you hit
Push through the water smoothly
As leaves drop subtly
On the surface reflected clearly.

Go my children,
Expect to capsize at some point
Lose you belongings, becomings, identity

Card-that tells you who you are.
Have to abandon thoughts, convictions
Your ship, then portage.
Carry only what you can hold
What is snagged on to you, drag.

Go my children,
Meet new playful
Exciting, terrifying friends
Whom you may only know
For a day but will stay
With you your whole life.
Take lovers along the way
Take many of them
Each will teach you something new
About you.

Go my children,
Dance in the rain
Smile at a puddle
Enjoy the sound of the word "drizzle."
And laugh at yourself
About the thought that dripped
Through the filter which strains
Your daily definition.

Go my children,
Live dangerously
Be careful not to be too cautious
Nothing is worse than living
Long because you took no chances.
Nothing could hurt your borrowed parents more
Than to think that they did not
Give you a sense of safety
To cross the lined
Streets.

Go my children,

Read books that you don't understand
Fly kites that you can no longer see
Give when you have very little
Be rich in more ways than one.
At least once be a friend to someone
Who has none
And run, just run!

Bless you my children,
Listen to all I have said
And listen to none of it
Live your life as a leaf
Falling from a tree
On a windless day!

Crow Party
Susan Gabrielle

Two crows
have a party
at the edge
of the muddy field road
where the weeds dip down low
toward straight rows of green

squawking, tussling
they tease
even though they know
I can't possibly face them today

more arrive to join their friends
passing out cups of cheap wine
and party hats
their funeral jackets tight
in the simmering sun

and I imagine I'll have a mess to clean up later
after you and I are done hiding
in opposite parts of the house

and even though I don't want to
I follow the sound of your voice
down the dark hallway
to the spare bedroom where you sit on
the edge of the single unmade bed

book open on your lap
you read to me about natural remedies
tell me we should be harvesting the corn silk
instead of stripping the cobs bare for market
since the sweet gold strings have healing properties
good for urinary infections, high blood pressure
bedwetting and inflammation of the prostate

and what I want to say
what I really want to ask
is why you didn't show interest
in such remedies
a year ago

when our son would have been born
why you didn't offer to make a trip
to the dry creekbed for
yellow dock (good for the blood)
or dig for
false unicorn root (to help with cramping)
or blessed thistle (promoting milk flow)
but then again, we didn't need that last one,
did we?

when I can speak
when I remind you of the date
you say only
Oh yes, I guess it was
and go back to reading

silently this time.

Father
Staci Fraley

It was like running down a hallway and having the door slammed in my face

I didn't expect it. It was all so sudden. So direct

I almost didn't want to understand what was happening

I wanted to be the innocent child that I was the day before, so gleeful and unaffected by the world around me

Life doesn't work out that way though, does it?

I wanted the feeling to escape from my mind so that the pain could fade away like the ember that veered from its flame

Instead, it felt like that flame was welling up inside of me and trying to shoot out of my mouth like a dragon that breathes emotions

I didn't understand what I was feeling, but I know it was somewhere between sitting in an empty cave that was decorated with a multitude of pictures that had to remind me what was happening, and being so pissed off that I could run away and never consider the consequences

I felt like part of myself had been stolen from me,
and there was no getting it back

The previous days had become a blur

A fog had settled in my mind the same way it does upon a mountain

Bits and pieces still peaked out, but the mass of everything was banished from reality

I felt alone

It was as if no matter what anyone said or did, that void had been cemented shut, meant to never be opened again

Years have passed, but the feeling still resides

I have blanketed it with distractions, but it still demands to be felt like a splinter that is too painful to remove

I will forever miss the protection I felt from his arms

The smile that reflected onto me just from seeing his

His voice that filled my soul with a love that can never be taken away

A love that was taken away

Flame Eternal
Kat V. Rosemond

For brother and sister 9/11 firefighters and EMTs

We are never too old and it is never too late to truly live...
Not while our eyes are open and we still draw breath.
Hope is a flame eternal
Faith is the sturdy stone pathway
Love is the greatest power in all the universe
Not even death can break or overcome it

Brothers and sisters of the firecross, lifestar, and shield
Keepers of the terrible little known tragic life-truths
Though the deepest dark surround us
Though death should snap with sharp cold jaws
Nothing can break our bonds
We are never alone

Take up the flame eternal
Keep your feet on the path of sure stone
Keep open the doors of your heart to the greatest power
Beat the dark walls that would hold and snuff you
Until they break utterly
And you are free and alive once more

My First Suicide
Carol Barrett

was Margo Bayne's mother. They lived in a big log house on Lone Oak Road. She kept the pine poles waxed and polished, from floor to roof. There was a little triangular landing where you could look down on everyone. Margo's Dad was an eye doctor and he'd be reading in the living room. Her brothers were never there, playing in the log fort they built in the woods near the main house. They were older than Margo and I felt sorry for her. She didn't have any sisters. I had lots.

Kathy was the oldest, with blond hair, mine is brown, and she always had two chopped egg sandwiches for lunch plus carrot sticks. The carrot sticks were very important. People said they'd give her good eyes.

I ate supper at Margo's sometimes because we were the same age. There were a lot of dishes and then dessert, some pudding with a fancy sauce you dipped from a little bowl with rosebuds. Mrs. Bayne was our Camp Fire Leader, and we'd troop over there, Kathy, me and the Crosby girls, to make booties for needy babies, and she'd correct the stitches. I had a pair she said we couldn't send, they weren't good enough. She said you had to think whether your own baby could wear them. I was ten and thought my baby would like them just fine. They took a lot of work, white with blue flowers.

What happened was, I was in the kitchen at our house and Mom was making a cake. I was licking chocolate beaters, and she told me since I was the one Margo's age, I might be hearing some rumors. She wanted me to know straight out. They couldn't find Margo's Mom the night before, all the dishes laid out same as usual. I figure Margo must have gone up to that little landing. You could see everything up there. We played dolls there, or jacks, or talked about the girls who wore bras. We didn't, not yet. Margo's Dad couldn't find her either. I got scared then. Margo's Dad was an eye doctor and he could see anything. She said Margo's Mom went down to some fort the kids built.

I was going to stop my Mom right then, tell her I knew all about the fort Margo's brothers built. We weren't allowed down there, no girls. But Mom had her eye on the batter real hard. She said Mrs. Bayne went down to that fort the kids built and shot herself before they all came home. Mom put the cake in the oven. I didn't want the beaters anymore and kept asking her why, you mean they couldn't take her to the hospital? Margo's Dad is an eye doctor and he should know what to do. The fort, the fort. I never saw any gun. What gun? We weren't allowed in there. They couldn't find her. Margo's Mom is dead. Now Margo's the only girl.

The next day at school I told Janet about Margo's Mom and the fort Margo's brothers built. I always told Janet everything. She said no, her Dad said it was a heart attack. That night we got out the paper to see for ourselves, and sure enough, it said Mrs. Bayne died suddenly of a heart attack at her home. It listed a bunch of stuff but didn't say Margo's Mom was our Camp Fire leader. I guess that's what my Mom meant, that I'd hear a lot of rumors. I wished the paper had at least told about the fort, even if they left out that part about the gun. I mean, that's where she went, it was not in her house with dinner ready.

Note: Originally published in *So To Speak*. Copyright held by author.

People in the Streets
Louis Hoffman

I want to rage
At the people in the streets
Walking with usual somberness
Not that extra I feel

Talking on their phones
Texting and reading messages
Checking sports scores

I am angry
Their eyes have not changed
They show no hallowness
Or redness from tears

They are just being
Their eyes remain alive
Unaffected, unknowing

You are no more.

Pink Rain
Paul T. P. Wong

Pink rain is falling so quietly
As cherry blossoms meet their fate.
My misty mortal eyes can only see
A grey mist outside the window panes.

Where are the boughs laden with flowers?
Where is the glory of sunny Spring?
The beauty that filled my heart with bliss
Now fills my life with misery and pain.

She came into my life as a shining angel
But vanished like a ghost without a trace.
The short-lived moments of happiness
Have all become painful memories.

Gone are the music and the laughter
Gone are my youth and youthful dreams.
I must be content with my solitude
Like a barren tree facing winter all alone.

This is how it will all end –
Without farewell and without tears.
I'll leave my earthly sojourn
For an everlasting Spring.

Lebkuchengewuerz
Katherine Kreil-Sarkar

A thousand or more moments are missing
from my being. Marzipan
sentiments. Candied expressions.
Inside my gingerbread house of lies,
I starve.
My chicken-bone fingers proof.
While carrion malice birds scavenge roof tiles.

My memories and patience frittered
away, leftovers mildewing.
My stability crumbling.
Moth eaten, my sanity.
The minions in the shadowed corners
of my consciousness, my helplessness
blatantly evident, creep
out and gnaw the royal icing foundations.

I, myself, the wizened crone, self-reviewing
for nefarious purpose.
Broken brittled heart.
Critical pieces scattered.
The flames of self-renewal are burnt out
and smoldering. Small
embers flicker threateningly,
wisps of change will extinguish or set ablaze.

Séance
Nesreen Alsoraimi

This séance comes without warning or
Calling
I am speaking to a ghost
You've been dead to me for a while
In obscure languages
Encrypted in both worlds
Authenticity may be lost
But I need it to feel close
Now I need it most
Need to adjust my compass
At a lamppost
that I wait at
that I stay at
I hear what you say
Smooth inscriptions
Delicate descriptions
Model worlds collapse
they disintegrate
as I build in the mud
as I plant and I wait
for this tree in the desert
to grow and take shape

Seeing You Die and Letting You Go
Monica Mansilla

Seeing you die was easy
letting you go was not
In the darkest hour of my life you left me
Yet the joy and peace of your departure filled the room with
the brightness of your love for me

Seeing you die was peaceful
As I held your hand and my ear rested on your chest,
I heard your last breath
The greatness of your life ended with the same peace and love
that you gave me everyday
Seeing you die was easy
Letting you go is not

You held me as a newborn
abandoned into the world
yet my heart knew no desire for greatest father
than the one you were to me
Yet my heart knew no desire for greatest love
than the one you gave to me

You taught me strength
You taught me love
You taught me wisdom
You taught me joy

In the last hour, in the last minute I whispered in your ear
"I will be ok"
Just the two of us
No tears, just love…
Holding you as you died was easy
Letting you go will never be

Sailing the world without you

Seems unnatural, it's not right
But the love you gave me and taught me
Will never change,
Will always nurture me,
Will never die.

Melting Snow
Michael Moats

Teardrops melting the freshly fallen snow
A favorite resting place for my old, fat dog.
Heat lamps, doggie doors, and an outside house
All options that you primarily saw as needless.

Demanding, intelligent, and loving.
Your disposition
A familiar one,
Like the other ladies in the home.

First the arthritis,
Then the breathing.
Nothing would stop you
From enjoying the child's play next door.

The barking subsided,
The pace had slowed.
Pleasurable groans
With the rubbing of your ears.

I saw your decline,
I saw your struggle.
Your still strong attitude and wagging tail
Had helped me avoid the decision.

The weather changed
And so did you.
Your stubbornness still present
Beneath the confusion and labored breath.

Wintery woods,
The peacefulness of falling snow,
Your favorite playground.
A good day to die.

I look into your eyes of love
Tired, yet comforted by my broken presence.
280 lbs of weeping flesh
Desire and understanding, in combat.

I share the broth
From my lunch with you.
At first, hesitation, before lapping at our bowl.
Most likely your giving, rather than want.

So tired, you lay
My breath, too, is labored.
Your head resting against my arm
As I rub your belly with memories of past.

Not ready to make the call
I want to prolong the day.
Loving you too much
To avoid it any longer.

My stomach knotted
Waiting for him to arrive.
Final private moments
Of love and old, puppy kisses.

You continued to speak to me
As you had so many times before.
You became silent and still.
I rubbed you gently long after.

Caressing your ears,
Stroking your fur,
And saying goodbye to a friend,
I walked you as far as I could.

Snow is falling,
Snow is melting,

An understanding that you already had.
No wonder you allowed it to blanket you.

To my old, fat dog
You have given your whole life to me.
Run free, my girl,
Run free!

Teardrops melting the freshly fallen snow...

Hospital Haiku
Tracy Lee Sisk

This series of poems was written in reflection of experiences while a loved one was on life support. ~ For Michael

Sad faces around
Solemn with what is unknown
Waiting for some news

Lungs stop when doc shows
All else fades away fast black
Breaths resume with news

Tubes pierce your body
The machine forces your breath
So rhythmic is its tempo

My heart drops at thought
Might this bout be the last one?
I surely hope not

Do you want to fight?
The doctor asked you today
How that must have stunned

You want to survive
You want to try to beat it
Good news to my ear

An Ecology of Grief: Haiku Collection
Virginia (Gina) Subia Belton

The Winter of Your Dying Time

Four full days and nights
We sit vigil, dwelling in
The house of our sorrow

Your house, *this* dwelling
Place, of love and forgiveness
Is fleeting respite

The tributaries
Of tears come together in a
Rising river flow

This dark winter night
You take your last breath, afterward
Owl flies past by your door

Ancestors rely
On these animal totems
And your soul leaves us.

"I believe in such
Things" whispered the hospice nurse
We turn in silence

Your mother, sisters
Tending to your lifeless form
And gently we bathed you.

Even as we wash,
Your life-force engulfs us all
In the dimly lit room

We three women breathed
You in, as if to inhale
Every last molecule

January fog
Dreams across your moist front lawn
You leave me brother

One Elder shrieks our
Sorrow into the grey sky
"Don't take him!!!!"… We yield.

Fulfil my duty
I lead, led by the hand of
Our ancestor's songs

The rain relentless
As we lower your ashes
Into lamenting earth

Spring, I surrender to My Grief

In the tender spring
Of our homeland, I pray for
Us to meet. Heart broken.

Sometimes I wake up
It is too much to feel you
I choose to sleepwalk

For a moment in
The sun, I almost forgot you're dead
Flowers remind me.

The Anguish of Summer's Heartache

Hot summer valley day
White roses for your graveside
Birdsongs trill rosaries.

Sliding down the burrow
Of my monastic silence
Tears, deep underground

I go out now and
Pretend that I am happy
This soothes the others

Some will say
There are seasons to our grief
If this is true I am dwelling

Fall's Crackling Transformation

Geese honking in the
Big Sky, robin sitting
Lightly on the path

Hung pictures today
Appears I can walk by "you"
Without searing pain

Gently I arrange
This alter of your images
Summoning "you" back

Walking by your photo
I can only glance from the
Corner of my eye

Birthdays, you and I
In the fall, I chance memories
Of our childhood

"Let him rest" our mother whispers, so I let you go.
From a delicate chain around my neck, I wear your perfect
  heart.
You speak to me now, from the wisdom seat of our Ancestors.

Nearness of You
Louis Hoffman

for Heatherlyn

It's not death
But the thought of missing you
That captures my heart with terror

Whether heaven or rebirth,
Or reunited with some
Reality unknown,
My existence would shine dim
Even in streets of gold
Without the nearness of you

The soft touch of your hand
The way your curves find a way
To touch in the night
Your laughter that fills my heart
While filling the room
That beautiful face
Soft eyes
And a soul
That gave me a home
Beyond the physical world

The loss of these
and so much more of you
Terrifies more than death,
Comforts more than life.

Can You Hear Me Tap
Tammy Nuzzo-Morgan

Can you hear me tap, tap
tapping on your window
pane, pane, pain dripping
puddles of maybes, what-ifs,
could-and should-have-beens
all pool, pull together
into thick slick, sickening grief.

I've been watching you
from that star
been listening to your tears
to your whispered prayers.

I did get to fly ma
see the Pacific at the
break of day
touched the wild Mustangs
in Colorado, told them your
name.

I returned to tell you
I'm safe and sound, so
go on live, find your peace,
your piece of the sun,
I am *still* your son.

Ode to an Old Woman
Marna Broekhoff

On a crystal august afternoon
We gather in the Glenn Starlin Courtyard,
A tapestry of ruby roses and sage of jade
Around firs set into velvet lawn,
Honoring her soul mate whose soul will never die.
Bugles of Canada geese beneath the sapphire skies
With unfailing direction trumpet the arrival of Miriam,
Our mother, earth mother, mother of us all,
On this, her 90th birthday.

Queen for a day, she shyly but regally holds court
While her throng of friends and family pay homage,
Receiving old men stooped over canes, elders even to her,
Young women with Nikes, just returned from Pre's Trail,
Recently-retireds, with recently colored hair,
Babies (her great-grandson) contented with pacifiers.

Do we honor her because she is our mother
(biological mother, soul mother)
Whose diamond-sharp eyes have perceived our virtues,
So often hidden among our warts,
And still held us up in her steadfast, loving gaze?
She has talked with me about my own mothering
(Alex's struggles), and my own mother (Ellen's snobbery),
Never leaving me defensive.
She has rejoiced in my successes as though they were her own.

Or do we honor her because she is still
The daughter of our youthful lusts for life,
Reading Jared Diamond's newest,
Attending Mozart at the Hult,
Weeding the rhodies behind her Sunset home,
And most of all, birthing her lifetime of collected poems
(titled *Wait a Minute*) on her nonagenarian evening?

We ponder such thoughts in this bejeweled courtyard.
The Ed Coleman Trio Plus One trumpets a life well lived.
Earthly shadows lengthen, and in the sky above,
The Evening Star suddenly twinkles like a diamond.
My beloved source of hope, wisdom, and stability,
Miriam Starlin, Mother Mir, I will always migrate toward you,
My North Star.

One Bare Place Setting
Louis Hoffman

One bare place setting
Quietly, filled with sadness
She is there no more

Trying to Manage
Aliya Granger

"I do want to discuss with you all, the option of a hospice and just go over all that that will entail. He doesn't have to go to a hospital or a nursing home at any time. A hospice can be in the comfort of your own home. The point of a hospice is just to make sure the person is as comfortable as possible before they prepare to --"

SLAM!
I run outside hurrying to get to my bus stop.
Pop my earbuds in and blast the most uplifting music I can find.
I get into the school,
Rush upstairs to poetry class,
Smile and laugh with the classmates.
I recite poetry like it's nothing.
As if poetry comes naturally.
As if poetry doesn't literally suck the life out of me at times.

I crack jokes with the teacher.
Smile as brightly as possible.
Masking the tears I cried right before coming to class.

Nobody knows what's going on.
I wish I didn't know what was going on.
I wish what was going on stopped.
I wish I could stop thinking of what's going on.

But constant conversations are taking its toll.
The agony is hurting me physically, mentally, spiritually, emotionally.
The loss of breath is taking mine away.
The pain I see is driving me –

My grandfather is dying.
And I can't do anything about it.
My grandfather is dying
And he doesn't want anybody to do anything about it.

18 years and the most I knew about my grandfather was that he was in the army.
Had no idea what war he fought in.
18 years and I knew that he earned a purple heart.
Had no idea what for.
18 years and I knew that his big thing was giving people a big thumbs up.
18 years!
And the day after I made it to my 19th year I found out that his time was coming to an end.

I live with him.
I see it all happening.
I live there so I know more than the rest.

My grandfather is dying.
And I'm just trying to manage.

The Heavens Cried
David Bentata

Went to a funeral today
On this dark, wet night
My friend is on his way now
To a New World of Light

The tears flowed all around
What do you say to an old father?
His sons, daughter and brothers
Let alone his aged, grieving mother?

He went too early
Tho' we know it must have been his time
Under our umbrellas and in our hearts
We felt he was still in his prime

There are no words
And when these fail, tears say it all
There was many a tear shed
As he was lowered amid the rain and squall

Your friends were there, man
More than you knew you had
You must have seen us all
Amid the intense sadness..... feel glad!

For if true riches can be counted
It's counted out in love from others
You left a millionaire, my friend
So many sisters did you have, so many brothers

You bore your illness with true courage
Gave hope to all and all in you showed their pride
Goodbye my friend on this dark night
When in its sadness.... even the Heavens cried.

The Ghost In My Abdomen
Candice Hershman

I awoke to a ghost
inside of my abdomen,
a hot ghost
made of desire,
unsettled as if
to contend with
unfinished business.

It walked
the halls of my arms,
the chambers of my heart,
ascending my ribs
rattling chains,
then hanging heavy
like a resigned child.
It could not find its bed,
and so it cried
to be embraced
by a surrogate organ,
to be relieved,
and wondered if
another little death
would provide assurance
or perhaps allow it
to be a quenched settler.
The ghost
finally became so tired,
it knelt down and slept
on the empty floor.

The ghost hoped
that if it could find a new place,
it would be a soul
once more.

Spirit
Robert A. Neimeyer

To a greater extent than most of my verse, this poem has a strong narrative structure, arising as it does from my therapy with an African American mother named Cara struggling with the death of her infant daughter at 7 months of gestation. As often happens for me, I found myself moved by an empathic bond with this woman's experience, so unlike my own. But unlike most of my therapy, from which I return imminently to the arms of my family, this first session of six was conducted in a distant city, and I returned to the contemplative anonymity of a hotel room. This poem bearing the imprint of Cara's story arose in that private place.

She was seven months in you
wrapped snug in your house of flesh
when she came to rest,
turned her face to the dark wall.
Beyond your high hard hope
you knew in your heart that she was gone,
this sliding shift of gravity
in your belly, in your bed.

You named her *Spirit*
because this is how she came to you—
there and not there,
a doll baby with eyes
painted shut. Instinctively,
your hands reach out,
grasp at air,
try to pull the light toward you,
into you, disperse the darkness.
A silent cipher, no one
can know what you have lost.

Now she stares at you
with the indifference of the angels
through the paper eyes, smiles

of baby pictures in your obstetrician's office,
the glazed gaze of newborns nursing
in restaurants at their mothers' breasts.
One after another, she tries on lives,
in the frames, in the arms of strangers.
She leaves each like a pair
of discarded shoes.

And so you seek her
in the misty maze to which she has retreated,
the shadow flash of dreams,
the sudden sightings of a body,
small and dark as a polished stone,
      and as cold.
Left still on the couch,
found wrapped in a box,
she practices dying until it is perfected,
until you find a new way

of holding on.

Over the Hill
Ted Mallory

You always told me to be careful on the downhill
it was easier to lose your footing and slip, you said

take your time
take it easy
enjoy the view
don't be in such a hurry
it's not a race

On the way up it was harder and slower
but I thought I was so strong and so tough

It made me proud
each step of the climb
I was accomplishing something

and I felt confident and safe, with you on ahead

but I was impatient
I couldn't wait to get to the top
I wanted to get to see what you could see

but when we peaked
you kept on walking
no time to stop and bask at the zenith

I lost sight of you for a minute
you below the crest on the downward slope,
me on the upward, still climbing, catching up and catching my breath

Now,
instead of seeing the dirt and rocks
and my own knees and boots,

I can see the panorama just like you promised
but I can also see you on ahead
descending descending
up where I can't be yet
but where I know I have to go

I can't enjoy the big picture
because I want to keep my eyes on you
and not lose you again
and because I see all the chasms and cliffs and crags
around you, behind you, beyond you
and right in front of you
things neither of us could see on the way up.

On the way up, I wanted to stop and rest because it was such a strain
now I want to stop and wait
because this feeling is so weak and worn and vulnerable
exhausted after so much strain on the way up,
but now we need our strength even more
we need our balance and agility more
so that we won't stumble and plummet to the bottom before we can reach it gently
but there's no stopping gravity and momentum
and time

I can see you far ahead
too far ahead
I want you up here by my side
I liked it better when you were here to catch me and to steady me
and to encourage me to keep going
to assure me that I could do this

I'd rather still be walking with you
but I can't just gallop and catch up to you
even though I want to be there to catch you and steady you

I wish you'd just stop and wait while I gradually catch up with you
but I'm scared to travel where you are

Downhill is definitely faster than uphill
but I'm not sure it's as fun
the trail seems to keep slipping out from under me.

I know that the pastures and waters you're headed for offer rest and reward
but between this mountainside and there seems so hard
and while the vista seems clear, twilight is falling
and I'm losing sight of you

Just promise you'll be there waiting at home
once I finally catch up

Many Years Have Passed
Laurie Phillips

Many years have passed since she left us
That cold dark day just before Christmas.
Seeing my mom hurting so bad
Was the most painful experience I have ever had.
The pain lessens with each passing year
It has now been replaced with memories I hold dear.
I wish I had spent more time with her;
But I moved away and only sent an occasional letter.
I think of my grandmother every time I smell lilacs in bloom;
She kept fresh cut flowers in every room.
And that smell of melting butter right before it browns in the pan;
I love to make her recipes whenever I can.
I don't want these memories to fade away
So I share them with others to make sure they stay.
When family gets together, we imitate her Polish accent
We are now able to laugh instead of vent.
My mom's mom, my sweet grandmother
Her memory is in my heart forever.

Armin's Shoes
Grace Harlow Klein

I saw Armin's shoes beside the mantle,
    Sitting there after he last wore them on Saturday.
Steve had polished them not so long ago.
    It is the first of many reminders
That Armin is no longer here.

I had a massage this morning.
    Theresa worked on my neck and shoulders
Trying to release the tension
    So tight it is affecting my voice.

I knew I needed to cry –
    But the sobbing went deep
All the way back to my age of fourteen,
    The day my youngest sister Jeanine died
And the days that followed
    When I was frightened, helpless, angry and bereft.
Finally there is an answer.

"Granny will make another book,"
    Said my granddaughter, Mairead,
In her childhood wisdom,
Linking her experience of the book I made
After the death of Junie, our much loved yellow lab,
    To that of her grandpa.
No longer helpless, only sad,
    I will have Mairead and Caitrin
And Katie and Jacob
    Make their own books about Armin,
Their sweet grandpa.

Finally my helplessness of long ago is transformed
    Into the creativity of preserving memories
Of the special person who was my husband.

And I begin a new link for my grandchildren
That beloved people – and dogs – live on
In the memories we keep of them.

Death Poem #22
Richard Bargdill

Her death

only left
the lonely

with less.

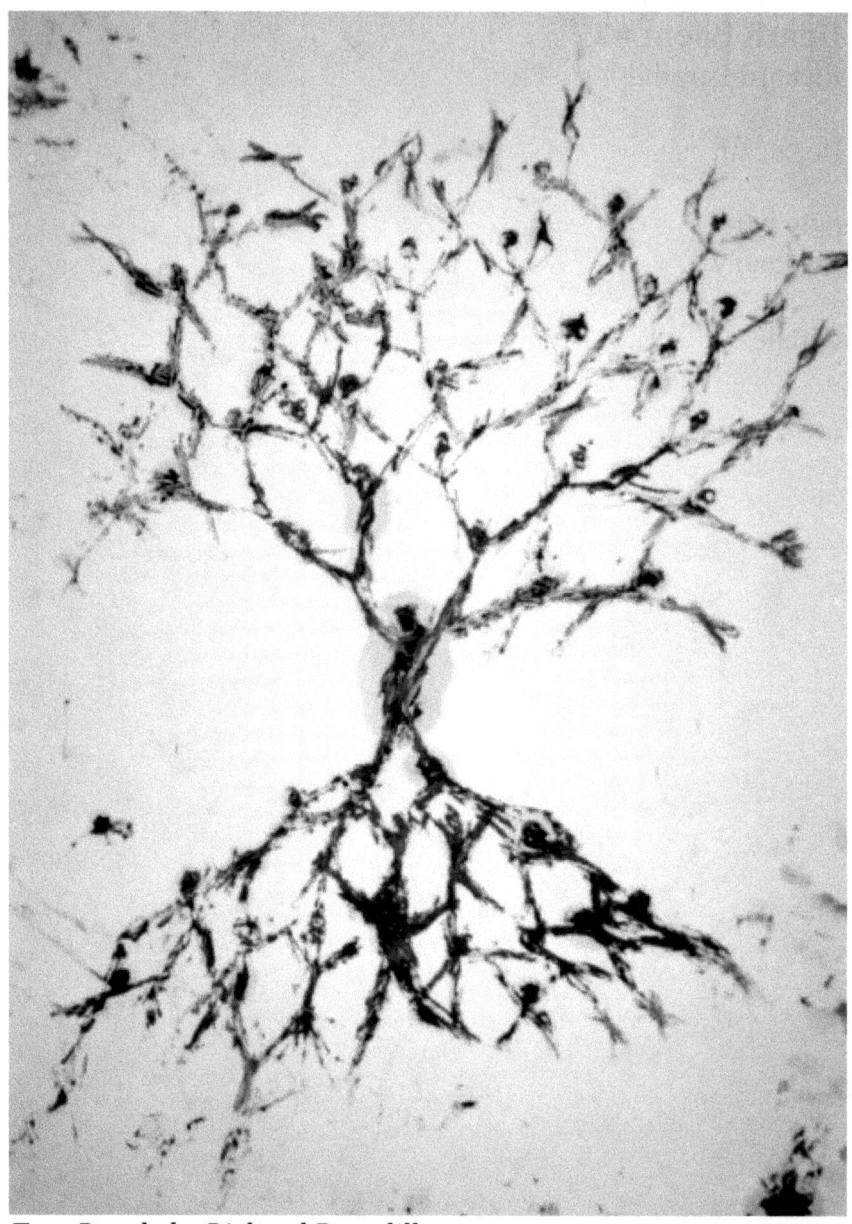

Tree People by Richard Bargdill

Survivors
Robert A. Neimeyer

Like some of my other verse, this piece reverberates with the intensity of my participation in the quest of clients to surmount impossible loss. But unlike my more narrative poetry, this one attempts simply to capture a long moment of emotional standoff in a couple pierced by the grief of a daughter's chosen death. In doing so, it tries to honor the individuality of mourning, while also acknowledging it is too frequently neglected systemic complexity. My intent was to speak to a part of these parents' pain, not to demean it with the saccharine reassurance of forced consolation.

He has stopped trying
to grasp her remoteness
that he mistakes for calm,
this cooling that accompanies
the wintering of her grief.

Since their daughter's explosive
departure, its echo
like a slammed door,
she has pulled in, and in,
away from the pain,

away from him.
What he cannot know is how
she slips inside the sleeve
of her music, the lyrics
of angels
        touch
              return,
draws down into the bubble
of her hope.

Alone in her car,
the music builds a room
around her, around the room

a house through which
she strolls.
It is in the nursery
that she feels the peace,
rocks her child, rocks herself,
restores the bond.

Too soon, the car turns itself
into her drive, slides
into the vault of garage.
Her hand finds the latch,
pulls her out. She takes the steps
like a condemned man.

The forced hello fades,
yields to the distance.
She glances up at him,
sees the eyes,
the terrible mirrors,

and turns again to stone.

Parts of Speech
Carol Barrett

in memory of Caroline Shrodes

Only two mornings since you gave in
to the ground, and I am hunting the green
nursery for signs, refusing any noun
but life. *Full sun,* the markers
advise, small instructions
tacked to their run-on sentence
of grief, like notes
in the margins of manuscripts, your bright
letters tugging the bloom.

Later I will walk the adjacent
years of our lives, subjunctive
rooms of talk, interjections
of fruit cups, participles
left to their own devices.
But here among perennial ivy,
baskets of periwinkle
and bougainvillea flash fuschia
like a verb in present tense.

Can you hear the lines ringing,
infinitives of friends,
the day's conversations splashed
with *Caroline?*

I stake out the evening
for poems: clusters of kalanchoe,
lipstick pink, and the deeper
hearts of begonias, the open grammar
of leaves. Kneeling to trowel,
I slip the soaked roots out
easy as parentheses.

The night breathes on. All sound
is edited now but that soft
cat-pad down the corridor
of seminars, your true-red
shoes, their rhinestone buttons
blinking like a perfect paragraph,
your gypsy smile like a preposition
in the sky: *of, with, beside, beyond.*

Note: Originally published in *The Network*. Copyright held by author.

Death's Courting
Louis Hoffman

Death
Why must you court me so
When you know I'm far from ready?
It is not that I resist you
(I do)
It is not that I hate you
(I do)

I feel you lurking
Around the corner
Following me
As if a stalker
I feel you
Hiding in my chest
Stealing a beat
Every now and then

I want to befriend you
When that time comes
To welcome you in
and share a pot of tea

It is not that you must
disappear
Just go away
For now

At night I cuddle with
my sons
Then lay with my wife
Each time
Taking in the touch
Nourishing the love
Knowing it is not time

Death
You must go
Leave me with my sons
Leave me with my wife
Once this life has been lived
Once I've been used up
Then you will be
Welcomed back
We'll have that cup of tea

But, for now, death
You must go
I will not receive you
Not yet

The Desert of My Youth
Larry Graber

I will never forget the naked sounds
The purity of the desert birds
At sunrise and sunset

My long walks and hikes
In the land of the Early Morning People
Resonating to my true purpose
healing my youth

Those visits
with my grandmother,
eating fresh grapefruits
from her tree
lemon yogurt
BBQ cod on a bagel

The kindness in her eyes
The warmth of her arthritic
Wrinkled hands

Eye to eye
Before cell phones
We sat

Compared notes
Discussed the values
of living a good life
    Of lessons past
    Of the next

I can still hear the birds
of that region
at sunrise
and I want to cry ...

Last March
We buried my Aunt Sue
Leaving the valley

I said goodbye

No more blood descendants
inhabit it's arid soils

My loss is amplified

The bird cries
Match my own

I bathe in memories
And I know my family
has left much behind

Though they are no longer
Held to this earth
The desert whispers
It's barren calls

A sound that warms my bones

Some day I will meet
It's indigenous people
Sit under the desert palms
And weep

Swimming for Treasures
Nance Reynolds

Beginning today without grandiose notions,
Longing arrives - uninvited, relentless.
this sea opens up before me,
Stepping over edges-
    stony and sharp...
I heed the summons.
Deepened currents carve patterns for a few seconds,
then...seconds turn to darkness...

Dense northern winds toss me carelessly- directionless.
now, hovering near the water's surface, no light for guidance.
this search... filled with mystery each stroke, each breath
Journeying without you.

Windward or leeward,
no matter, no choice
dive, jump, roll, skip, creep or...
throw – myself in.
Toward some touchable memory of you...

I swim hard for miles – desperation fills lungs
    Will I find you?
    Incorrigible, unstoppable, tossed no more,
I dive deeper into the darkness unafraid and then....

Water turns to silk- silk, glimmering with light- wrapping me,
air fills deflated lungs with plenty,
Sensing an illumined grace, now
revealing form... barely ...of the love.

Relief breathes me in - as vacancy stirs and shifts,
    holding you, no longer am I trapped so tightly.
    desire waxes and swimming begins again, hard swimming,
seeking a chest of treasures now... seeking.

no matter, no choice
the precious gift finally emerges, or is it delivered?

A tear.
the found memory of you, heartfelt and swelling.
I swim gently now, in this ocean of tears...
   ever so softly.

The Boy They Love
Lisa Vallejos

Two women sitting
On the deck of a pool
A hot summer day
Laughing like old friends
At an inside joke
To onlookers it likely seemed ordinary
Nothing spectacular about either
On the surface

The one thing they shared
That brought them together
That changed them both forever
For one, a diagnosis
The other, an accident
Both, a heart

Those two unremarkable women
Linked forever through
Tragedy
Triumph
Love
One who gave the unimaginable gift
That continues to beat
In the chest of the boy
They love.

Reptile
Nesreen Alsoraimi

Each day that inches by
I shed another layer of you
And toss it aside
The memories still strong
Your hold on me is not gone
I look at the scales beneath me
And wonder what had kept me there so long
Hard for me to move
I let the absence of momentum
Lead my day
I've lost my way
Cant breathe
Cant believe
I am grieving once again
Tears I choke back
Odds are stacked too high
I grab at nothing
Muffle my prose
Afraid to expose
The sickness I hold
Waiting inside, in droves
There are fictional groves
Tangled and overgrown
I rest in between
In a hammock
In a cove
In my bed
In my head

Black Coffee
Catherine Granger

These days taste like black coffee;
Bitter, dark, eye-opening, burning my tongue.
Such a difference to the vanilla latte days,
I am so used to, that I crave.
But I will take it as it is,
No artificial sweeteners, no creamer to mask the taste,
Nothing to soften the blow.
Perhaps I will find comfort
In the harsh truth.

Hell's Gate
Kat V. Rosemond

As an EMT arriving at Pentagon Ground Zero 9/11

Gates of Hell yawning wide
Exhaling breath of smoke, burnt debris, fiery death
Jagged teeth protrude all around
Melted windows, twisted guts of structure
Where solid, strong walls and halls once stood.

I stand before the black, smoldering mammoth
Small...oh, so small am I
With my two little hands curled in defiant fists at my sides.
What am I against Hell's Gate?
What can I do against such Evil?
The world as I knew it is utterly shattered as is my soul,
Memories smolder on the ground

Phantom screams rip through the air...
Voices of the burning, voices of the dying yet hang in the smoke
I can hear them...
I can hear them...
I sense the ominous vibration in the air
Terrible roaring of crashing engine, rock, steel, pipe, metal, bone
Guttural rumblings of trembling earth
I can feel it...
I can feel it...

Broken bones, splinters of building, plane, and life
Mangled memories and dreams
Flow out with the river of ashen water
As blood from deep wounds
Across the ground, across my boots
Where I stand, with my crew at my sides
Rooted to the spot, gaping at stark Evil

Yet small as I am, I'm a child of the Light
Though my heart is broken and my soul cries within
In union with the suffering hearts and souls around me
I draw the breath of Life
Small as I am, I am one
A tiny, yet visible light amidst this bleak Darkness
With the heart lights from my crew beside me,
And my people all around in this deathly, tragic place
Giving their all, body and soul, to help.
The Shadow will not take me; not today!
Evil will not prevail.
Take heart and have hope.
Through Hell's Gate, our light will shine forth!

The Weeping Tree
Erica Palmer

I sat down under the willow tree
So surprised to feel it crying for me
Can this tree care? Can it count the cost?
The nearest human cannot sense my loss.

I drink from its perfume,
I taste of its wine;
Attempts to fill a longing
Lost so deep in time.

The light is real;
Darkness is too.
And the tree,
It also cries for you.

The "Crestone Experience"
Juanita Ratner

This poem was written after the author moved to Crestone, CO, a tiny town in the Sangre de Cristo Mountains. Crestone is renowned as a spiritual center, home to many traditions: a Carmelite monastery, Zen monastery, Tibetan Buddhist sanghas, Sri Aurobindo Center, and Haidakhandi Ashram among them. The Crestone area had been sacred to Native Americans, whose shamans would go up into these mountains on vision quests. Perhaps elements of the poem speak to the feeling of being in transition of any kind.

Is this what it's come to?
My heart screams
Searing with pain
Clutching in fear
To what?
Nothing to grab hold of
Nothing solid
Anymore

Dissolving.
Am I to die here
Or-worse-go mad
In this, what was to be
My moment and place
Of glory
Integration, culmination
Of these many years
On the path.

Thrust instead
Into obscurity

And yes, at first my heart
Understood
I groped in the dim cloud,
Acceptant.

I had heard about this cloud
I quickly learned to find my way
Sign by sign, moment by moment
As Life revealed Herself to me

Her secrets - unspeakable
Her treasures - ungraspable
Only to be found
Moment by moment
In the obscurity of this hidden place
Hidden way
Ordinary life
Illuminated
By the light
Revealed
Therein.

And yet

Surrounded by all this treasure
I
Feel
Tossed wave upon wave
Lost
In a stormy sea
Of me

Waves of nothingness
Crushing me
Melting me
Squeezing out every excruciating breath

I
Searching desperately
For what
I
Can never see

My true purpose
Unique destiny
Gathering itself
By the very force
Of the death-throes
Of this
I

The phoenix stirs
So - there still is life
What remains
In this clump of ash
The debris
After the storm moves on

It collects itself
And waits
Surely somewhere
Something asks my help to be born
The soul behind the Voice
That beckoned me here
Will reveal itself

I walk on
The giant peaks bless me
Wash me
Fill my spirit
With their power

And I know
When the moment is right
My very being will respond
Appropriately.

First published in *Searching for My Real Self*, © Juanita Ratner, 2005

At Grandma's Feet
Lisa Vallejos

She taught me how to make a bed
Tamales, Tortillas & chile
the proper way to fold a fitted sheet
Everything I needed to know
I learned at Grandma's feet.

She modeled for me compassion
Kindness, courage & humility
How to treat a stranger
How to be a decent human,
I learned at my grandma's feet.

She taught me to laugh
And how to be alone
She lived so meager, yet complete
I learned what really matters,
At my Grandma's feet.

When it was time, she went so gracefully
On her terms, the way she wanted
Beautiful and bittersweet
I learned how to die with dignity,
At my Grandma's feet.

Vicissitudes
Shelley Lynn Pizzuto

It is here in this silence
Cast into the light between the shadows that stretch of the then and now
Warm and wet with wonder flows within
Here in this silence
This sanctioned womb
Dynamic strands collected through the dust of fractal history
Binding forms that tempt surrender to the ineluctable mystery
Existence
Open enter and expand
Touch here, yes, where the leader and the lure form of the
Deity, the flux and sustenance

In between awareness
Pushing through our meetings with insatiable appetites
We crave to create new reflections, of all that we dare not be

Navigate this tide dear child
As you will push to find reason and drown again
Illusions
For underneath where it is wound there is no wound that is of permanent matter
You will not break in there
Tempted is the pressure of birth as the thread is pulled that spins you out
Grieve child
Push the petals to their bloom
For it is only here that you will come to lose your mind to that which you are not
Emerge

Tractor Ride
David Bilyeu

for Ellyn

Enough of the illusions, schemes for more, friends who aren't
Instead, buy a hazelnut farm in the Willamette Valley
shell nuts and stay warm on wet days while tending the roaster.

We could trade in one life for another,
      picking one Thoreau inspired
      where the antidote for backsliding into
      haste and accusations - why can't you...
          why didn't you...
          how come you...
          and did you really.....?
      is to retire to the opening in the glade
      find figures in the towering white clouds -
      a racing Pillsbury Dough Boy pursued by the Big Bad
        Wolf.

      We cheer the wolf.

Daylight slips away
      we walk to the old barn
      crank up the old grey '51 Ford -
      it never did have a fast life -
      The putt-nup, putt-nup
      is less motor power than movement by hiccup,

and share the cupped-hand, metal seat like motorcycle mates;
your chest expanding against my back with each
      breath
your head heavy with thoughts of loss and pain
      against my shoulder.
Treads, cross-hashed, lay herringbone prints down the darkening
ways
between trees in symmetry and boughs all the same height.....
I lean, you lean, but twigs and leaves collect in our hair for
sylvan crowns.

At this pace, the dogs trot easily port and starboard,
vanilla colored beams from the old headlights spot their wagging
tails
like moonlight on a ship's wake.
The steady
         putt-nup
         putt-nup
         putt-nup

- takes us to a time when these trees were seedlings, the
  tractor knew no
         rust, and we.....we
         knew no grief.

Sharing Grief

This is a series of poems written within a call and response dialogue as part of a workshop on Culture, Trauma and Healing. The first was the call poem, the remaining were in response.

Mudflat Grief
Tracy Lee Sisk

My heart, a place of grief and sadness
Bumpy and smooth, wet and dry
Puddles, pools, and streams of tears on
The mudflat of my heart

Gulls, ducks, pipers, and cranes
Pecking up fresh images and feelings
The Frisco Bay swelling to heal and protect
The mudflat of my heart

Vessel of the Soul
Kat V. Rosemond

Mud and water
Elements of Earth
Elements eternal
The sacred building blocks
Of life

Mud becomes flesh
Life begins
Nourished by water
Caressed by the wind
Warmed in the sun

Flesh
The vessel
That holds the soul

Takes the sacred life journey
And at the end of the path
Flesh returns
To mud
Amidst the river of tears
Carrying the soul home

Mud Falls
Larry Graber

Mud gathered
on my boots today
A little wet
A little cakey

I could feel the earth
Uneven
And, I walked
Different

Same gate
with a feeling
something's there
under my step

No need to take it off
but I know it's there

I take another step

And a bit
more mud
drops away

once wet
now dry
and fading

in my boots
I hike another day

I feel the sun
catch yesterday's mud
As the outlines
of my boot
soles return

Mud falls away
there is more freedom

Mudflat by the Bay
Larry Graber

Mudflat at bay's inlet
I watch seabirds gather
Water shrinks away the shoreline
To dry land

A lone egret ...
Perched
on a dirt ridge

I have walked that trail
many times

Even a powerful sea
has it's refuge
A place for contemplation

Here there is no salt spray

The mud folds unto the land
Collects thoughts and memories
So many passersby

There is room here

You can place your
feelings in the mud

In the mud
Your feelings
are safe

The mud does not move
Opens it's arms
To hold your grief
And dry your tears

Can even dry
Your pooling eyes

Mud just listens
No interference
No attempts to fix pain

Here the rain is caught
Set free into the air
And Floats away

Nature's way
recycling

Today I walked
the mudflat path
Yet I stayed inside

Another brought
It to me

To share its power

Her grief held
In the mudflat

Released to the bay
and
Shared in our
Small group union

Together
In the mudflat

Our hearts
Were opened

Our losses
One loss

A shared poem
A shared voice

Death came into
The room
And brought
Life

All I Have is Silence
Paul T. P. Wong

Silence
Growing,
Expanding,
Filling my heart,
My life, my room,
And every available space.

Silence.
Not a sound,
Not an echo,
Not a hint of falling tears,
Not a sign of breathing,
Just the cold stillness of death.

Silence.
In the depth of silence,
In the silence of the night
I say a final goodbye
To all my dreams and pains,
Without burial and funeral.

Silence
Growing,
Expanding,
Connecting with all the lonely souls
Till a ray of sunshine
Penetrating the dark silence.

I'm So Sorry
Ted Mallory

You're dealing with so much
I feel afraid to offer any commentary
because I don't want to risk
offending you
or say anything
that will compound your pain

I want to say things
to heal
or help

but I know
nothing can
and I don't want
anything that could be beneficial eventually
to be trivial or superficial or even insulting
because it comes at the wrong time.

I've been here before
in the line
at the viewing
or the luncheon
after the entombment
not knowing what to say
or how to say it
not wanting to put you through this
not even sure
how much eye contact
to make.

But I've been someplace
like where you are now
I know not the same place
but someplace cold

isolated
on display
in front of
what seems like
a never ending
stream of well wishers
yet so alone
aching
aching
aching
so that you just want
to be left alone
but under sedation
put into a coma
so that you
don't have
to deal with it
anymore

I'm sorry
so sorry
not only for your loss
but because
I have no idea
what to say
or how to say it

I'm here
if you want me
but I won't be
if you don't
I just wish
I could tell which
because
it doesn't see fair
to ask you
to have to tell me
one way or another

I'm so sorry

Approaching Death
Louis Hoffman

Words cradled in loving arms
In this, the last embrace
Touch fades through rubbery skin
    Gray strands run smoothly along fingers
    Images of childhood reversed, as
    Comfort through the old eyes of a child

The deepest whispers are those not heard
...only felt
Presence,
Offering comfort no words could provide
Tenderness,
Eyes softly touching a heart
Freedom,
Life no longer fought for
..as a tired soul released

    The wish to say goodbye, now
    Not later
    Not as harsh wish, merciful
    A wish to die when not alone
    While fearing the near departure
    Mama, say goodbye today
    And let me be the warm face
    As you "go gently into the dark" embrace

In Trees Again
Victoria J. Hamdi

Tell me that you've died.
Affirm this nightmare,
Because I can't.
I'm calling to you,
But unbothered you walk away.

Ignoring that life no longer exists.
Running through this town,
People cannot hold you,
And your cries silent.
You have no idea
Of where you exist here.
You find solace in the company of birds,
Among branches of dead birch trees.

I don't want to speak of it,
But I feel I must.

I need you to know-
That expiration is your status.
And I cannot hold you anymore.
Speak-acknowledge-
Let me know you understand!
Because I cannot reach you
From where you are.

Choosing to Turn
Michael Moats

She is no longer *here.*
No taste.
No taste.
No taste.
There is no *fucking* taste to anything anymore.

The flavor of life seems to have vanished.
I am pissed off.
At God, at her, at the dealer.
For me they are currently one and the same.

No boundaries.
No labels.
They are all responsible for my pain.
My pain!

The pain that leaves this smiling shell empty on the inside.
Pretending.

Pretending?
Seriously?
Is this what I choose for myself?
No!
I did not choose this.
It was chosen for me…..by them!
By them!

Why didn't she just say no?
Why didn't she just turn away?
It had too much of a hold on her.
And, he kept giving it.

It wasn't her fault; it was his.
He just wanted his share.

But, he got more.
He got her life too.

Why didn't You stop her?
Why didn't You intervene?
You could have made her choose differently.
You could have saved her.

What?
What do you mean, why didn't "I" stop her.
I tried, but she couldn't hear me.

Why didn't I intervene?
I did, but she ignored me.

Why couldn't I save her?
You know her...she was a stubborn, spirited, pain in the ass woman.
God, I loved her!

I just wish she had made a different choice.
I wish she could have seen the opportunities that she was blind to.
I wish she knew how strong she really was.
I wish she had made a different choice.
A different choice...
A different choice...

....

Hmm....choice.
....

God, I feel so empty.
I'm tired of pretending.

Why don't You stop this?
Why don't You intervene?
Why don't You............

I am the dealer?
I am the choice?
……………………..

I don't understand.
………………………………
………………………………

Hmm, I am *my* dealer.
I am *my* choice.
……………………..
………………………………

I don't know where I'm going, but…..

I am going to choose.
I am going to turn.
I am choosing to turn.

I'm turning……..

I'm scared.
…………………..

God?!

Road Kill
Nesreen Alsoraimi

I watched you disintegrate
Day by day
Like road kill on the side of a street
It got unbearable
I had to turn my face
But I had to stay
I had to stay
And as you decomposed
I watched the remains
Blow in the wind
A piled of dust
in the end
Now I can only visit the man I knew in my memories
Because he's gone
I mourn his loss
I mourn his cause
I mourn his loss

Alter
LeesaMaree Bleicher

you have to assume it will alter you
love   you dream is like this

you would think that   it would be like rain
wet and softening your bones

like how when as a child you lay still as the morticians muse
how   after   the pain became your bones
then became   the way you breathed
until you were a teen

then you learned that you could cause the pain
then it was so much easier
to dress love as a tattered torn starving scarecrow
and believe that you were the dress you wore
and
the color of the lipstick
that promised   pretty in pink

a thousand lifetimes becomes   every fantasy   every failure

you gave up then   rushed the wind
as if it could reinvent you
instead you blew up like   the outdoor movie screen   where
you spent many a summers evening your face pressed into the
vinyl columns of a 56 Chevy's interior
your thoughts   his

a thousand lies, a thousand boys
flesh   eggplant bruised
summer came
goodbye   said hello

now   it is more like air
love

became
the color of your eyes
the sweep of your speech
your hand holding mine
your lips silencing the sorrow
of a thousand cold summers

knowing

i am still being held hostage by the Winter Queen
in midnights graveyard
wearing   a crown of crimson crows

Unfinished Narrative
Joy L. S. Hoffman

To the young child
Stripped from birthplace and culture
No biological mirror
Just a number and no name
As parents get the fame
Saviors they call them
Plucking you from destitute
The price is high
Because inside you die
Just a little each day
Life is missing something
And you just want to name it
But saying it out loud seems
Selfish
Petty
Pointless
Ungrateful

You may never know your story
And it may never know you
Family is redefined
On someone else's terms
But you have to embrace it
It will be the only family you ever know
Unless you choose to be
Selfish
Petty
Pointless
Ungrateful

And inside you die
Just a little each day
Life is missing something
And you just want to name it

The Cross Culture Citizen
Eylin Margarita Blake

She is a transplanted Peruvian with different rules, norms and numbers in this new land that she calls home.
By marrying her husband, she was inserted into the system of many doors.
During the process of obtaining her legal papers, she was stripped of all her personal information.
Throughout meetings with lawyers, doctors and government officials, this woman was able to fit into the government's outlines.
Now, she's been squeezed into a couple of pages on a form in the government's file.
She has been born again with Social Security number, driver's license, nine-digit telephone numbers starting with area code.
She is prepared to obey the system's law.
She has the ability to vote in this modern society.
There, people are special.
They have dissimilar personalities and cultures.
She respects everyone no matter what socioeconomic class they are in.
She is taking classes to become a vital part of her community.
She cares for her family.
Does she have freedom to be her own individual?

Only Here & Only Now
Samuel Ballou

Just when the moment has come and gone
Along the path of time we walk in this life,
Collecting memories that are no more;
Knowing that the unknown is yet to come
How long it seems, yet is so close
Ill prepared for the now; that is neither the *prior* that we
   tenderly hold onto,
       nor the *yet to come* that we illusion as real;
Love finds its place in the between of these two *ignes fatui* of
   our minds;
Love and embrace the moment that is neither the *prior* that we
   tenderly hold onto
       nor the *yet to come* that we illusion as real ...and...
Suddenly we find ourselves truly in the place of no time,
       where we can just BE...

The Dam Cannot Hold
Amelia Isabel Torres

Inspired by the "Expansion" scultupure by Paige Bradley and my own dark night of the soul.

Here I sit
broken in the sunlight
My scars illumined
from the inside out
Cracked

Bandages once invisible
hold together
fragile skin, bones, and breath

My light is showing

A bumble bee bumbles overhead
Scanning me
zzzzz
My scars shiver
revealing where they are hidden
Can he sense my shadows
quivering deep beneath
my ragged walls?

I crumple

liquid fear
seeping out
warmed by the sun

The bumbling bloke
bounces into the window
sending shockwaves skipping
across the glass trampoline
Disoriented

or giddy in his own delight
he shoots off
and I remain
Quaking

Light pools beneath my aching fractures
enflaming the cracks
searing the transparent tape
This dry dam cannot hold

What happens when the light breaks free?
Where will all my pieces go?
zzzzzz

Letting Go
Ericka Pate

dark hours fill with unrelenting anxiety
owning a pain so profound
no bottle of distraction can drown
    Assaulting anger
    Revealing insecurity
    Letting go
the hole in my heart your passing created
an aching puncture wound
a constant stream of tears cannot heal
    Assuaging grief
    Releasing sorrow
    Letting go
repeated days of mindless wander
falling back into unfulfilled routines
embedded in fragile defense
    Abating weakness
    Rebuking fear
    Letting go
a flood of isolated moments
consumed by the depth of loneliness
healing words go unheard
    Adopting indifference
    Rebuffing guilt
    Letting go
a strained look into my future
gathering a life's worth of faith
to venture down a path without you
    Abandoning strife
    Refunding hatred
    and finally…
    Letting go

Thirst

Emily Lasinsky

Lap 1,000.
Running in circles, getting thirsty.
I can see a clear glass of fluid on the outside of the perimeter.
Steadily running, steadily reaching,
Arms extended, face down.
I pass the glass with every lap, every lap more tempting than the last.
I can no longer feel my legs, or distinguish if I'm moving.
My breath is a song…overplayed.
My body is a resident…overstayed.
Time passes, but nothing changes.
The glass, still   beyond my reach.

Moving fast forward in slow motion,
My senses are overwhelmed.
The trees argue at their town hall meeting,
Animals rush to find a safe haven for the night,
The wind wrestles, nestles, and soothes.
Through all the noise,
I hear and feel a "Crack!"
The sound of my soul's case collapsing.

I long for something…
Water! I need water!
Why can't I reach the glass?
If there's a lesson I'm supposed to learn, I'm not going to live to learn it,
If there's something I need to turn around, I'm not going to have the strength to turn it.
Darkness.

Light.
The ground is wet, but the scent of dry leaves fills my nostrils,
This is not where I have been.

Frantically wondering where I am, I see the glass before me,
Enough liquid for me to survive.
As much as I want to guzzle it down, I'm filled with contemplation.
    What if it's not water?
    Should I drink and hope for the best?
    Should I decline and continue on my blind quest?
It took so long to reach what I thought I wanted,
but now I'm not so sure.
Am I even thirsty?
Lap 1,001.

Cloak of Happiness
Chelsea McCarty

Tear after tear I drowned in sorrow,
Hoping to wake to a better tomorrow.
Thoughts and thoughts picking at my head,
Reminding me how scared I am to be dead.
The anxiety kicks in and I start to shake,
These horrible feelings I just cant break.
It's killing me inside but they don't see,
Because on the outside I'm just happy little me.

Pushed into the Wilderness
Monica Mansilla

Took seven years and some month to detach from who I
thought would always be.
Uninvited open doors pushing me forward into the wilderness,
of a new land
Left the cold and fresh air that once was home
Faced the warm and terrifying landscape of the desert
My life was suddenly reduced to three full bags

No pictures in my suitcase
No reminders of what couldn't be
Just a bunch of chattered images
Of the dreams that I once build

I know no one…there are no trees
My apartment lacking windows
Have to cover down my knees

Family says they miss me
Yet no one knows if I am well
They condemn me for not trying
Don't they know I simply can't?

Always strong and independent,
but this time I need to know
that they miss me and they love me
I am not home
I need them more
I am grieving dreams
I am tired
I am facing life alone

Room
Robert A. Neimeyer

The evening before my departure for an invited address at a conference honoring my tragically deceased friend and colleague, Michael Mahoney, I sat in my study contemplating what I would say beyond the formal presentation. But rather than sitting at my desk or in my reading chair, as I typically would, I ensconced myself on a small divan on one side of the room, musing as midnight overtook the quiet house whose other residents had been asleep for hours. The conjunction of the empty space— visually devoid of its familiar inhabitant—corresponded with an inner emptiness, a quiet space in which the poem took shape. The poem began with its title, its double meaning suggesting a deeper reading.

Even the chair defines you
by your absence.
It lifts its arms
to embrace yours, opens its lap
to cup your form in its soft shape.
      Without you,
it is an empty hand.

On the footstool the books
mill in their randomness,
forget their call to common purpose.
The pens on your desk
have bled dry of words.
Your tablet is a tombstone
without inscription.

This is how we are cast
by the long light of your shadow,
persist in our objective irrelevance.
Collectively, we have lost
the threads of memory,
of intention, dropped the beads
from time's limp string.

The clock's pulse
measures the silence
like a tin heart, registers
only hours *since*, never *until*.

Slowly we are hollowing
ourselves through our grief,
as rocks are carved by sand
in a hard wind.
When we have let go of enough
of what we were
and grow perfect in our nothingness,
we will at last find an end
to the yearning,
and finally

have room for you.

Growing
Molly Kruger

I was as happy as I could be
Just my love and me,
With our handmade house and dinner –
Looking over the river.

He said once upon a time ago,
In that handmade house,
That unless something had time to grow –
It would always be false.

So he and I grew,
More and more each day
To get everything we ever knew we worked –
But also left room to play.

We built everything we ever had,
We were strong,
In that house we were glad –
Nothing could ever go wrong.

But that in itself is adjust,
For he and I,
We lived on trust!
But everything that lives to grow must die.

His name is now carved in stone,
And he has left me to grow alone.
But how is one to grow –
When their broken hem needs a simple sow?

I am done not knowing whether to keep on growing,
But since you have been gone,
You are the only thought I have had from dusk until dawn.

You are what the Lord gets
And the Sun never sets –
Without me praying to be back in your arms.

Because I was as happy as I could be
Just my love and me,
With my handmade house and dinner –
Looking over the river.

Hollow
Ashley Finley

I am hollow.
Empty.
The core of me poisoned and ripped out.
There is nothing here anymore.

And to the child I may never have.
Forgive me for all the times I said I would never have you.
The times when I
said that you would never exist.

I was foolish then.
Little girlish then.

Head full of lofty dreams
And selfish idealism.
I always thought I had a choice.
Always knew that motherhood would be my decision to make.

But,
Last week
I sat alone and barefoot in a hospital gown
Staring at a man who looked like God
As he told me, be careful what you wish for.

Cause sometimes selfish prophecies
Can become self-fulfilling prophecies,

He said,
because I had told myself so many times that I would never want you,
My body finally decided to believe me.

Hostile uterus,
Building walls that may never house you
Fortifying my womb against you.
Threatening to kill me, if I ever broke my promise.

And the only cure,
Was to set off atom bombs inside me.
Make a wasteland of your future homeland.

So,
I said yes.

And it hurt.
And now I am just a mass
Of regret, and sadness, and nausea,
And hurting muscles, and salty tears,
And falling out hair.

I think I am being punished
For denying you before I even knew you.
But the man who looks like God
Tells me I made the right choice.

And all I can think
Is how I don't want to be hollow anymore.
I hope that one day,
You decide to give me a chance.
Baby, I take it all back.
I want you.

Surviving the Loss
Carrie V. Pate

Truth overwhelming-
Pain from the joy you knew or somehow missed
Reality overturned-
Chaos impossible, order unthinkable
Swimming in a dense fog-
But you can't escape, so you struggle
And you struggle-
And struggle-
And the world spins as recklessly as ever.
But you don't-
Unmoved, unmovable, trapped, but unfortunately still breathing
Painful, unwanted
Thoughts, feelings, emotions, crushing, and numbness
Swimming toward the shore-
The shore you once knew well, but not anymore
It's not the same reality-
You've seen the other side of things
Within the doughy mist-
Beneath the swirling waters that still grasp at your feet
You make your way inland-
Always looking back, visions of the sea fading
Leaving the memory-
In images, sharp pangs of feelings without warning
Lost with your loss-
Lost with part of you, the part that you traded
To carry your grief

Snowfall
Carol Barrett

A few days before I die
I'll shovel a thin ribbon
along the muffled walk
where old flowers
merge their snowy heads
in the thickening bed.
I'll stroke the library banister
long way down to the basement floor,
the record player spinning
its scratchy hymn. The "girls"
will be taking off their scarves,
unrolling thick beach towels
on the beige carpet, each
in her own space. I'll go
to the head of the class, greet
each pink face like a new poem,
begin with a shoulder roll, a brisk
whirl of the hands. Midway
we'll stop to rest. Someone
will put water on in the kitchenette.
I'll remember my grandmother,
rising each morning from the yellow
chenille to sit-ups on the hardwood
floor, then teach the younger women
things which pulse through us
when the shape of hips no longer
matters. We will coach each other
past funerals and broken wrists,
our bodies warming the chattering air.
Someone's granddaughter
will be visiting, her braids long
as the scarves. We will take turns
saying how quick she catches on,
her waist bending to a tender

compass. After the last
curled spine extends to the top
of the hour, we will sip tea
and stories, then pass through
the upper chambers where new books
gloss the round tables, my hands
pressed to the glass door
like a prayer, mittens disclaiming
imprint, the squeak sounding behind me
as the indelible snow takes over.

Note: Originally published in *Christianity and Literature.* Copyright held by author.

I mumbled
Anne YJ Hsu

I mumbled "...okay", when she asked to take you there and then.

I let her,
I handed you over,
Even as you starred at me in disbelief.

I froze.
You struggled and fought.
The car door was shut,
She started the car.

I stood still, looking out the window from our couch,
with my hand over my mouth as she pulled away.

Echoes of you wailing swept the driveway.

Unnamed
Tammy Nuzzo-Morgan

for Joey

Sometimes I can see him, the one who could-have-been, our
   boy.
Your sea-green eyes, velvety brows, tall & dimpled chin,
   blended
with my full lips & curly hair; so full of possibility.

His birth date is fast approaching. In high school: baseball,
wrestling, poetry?

He, the magician who fooled the Universe, didn't desire to
   travel the dark tunnel
to cold air, bright light. Didn't think the show was worth the
   price of admission,
the one who told us to go on, live without him.

Alzheimer's Disease
Erica Loberg

Like a child
An old friend
It takes over the
Eye
Of the beholder

The beloved.

And sucks itself
Back
Into the lids
It takes hold
Of the ebb and flow of the
Of human exchange
The death unleashes itself onto
Two ends of the spectrum

Yours and mine.

And you sit in it
You become it
You be it

Alive in a lost world
Alone in a new world

A slow ride down
Dante's Inferno
To the end of all ends

An old life
Now
Gone

Now
Unknown
Now
Lost

Where the known alive life
Is dead

And...
The tears become stone
The cries become moans
The sick become unknown
The pain of forgetting
The truth of dying

Finds its way home.

The Lost Home
Monica Mansilla

But once…I had a home…
I knew that it was real and I knew that it was true
and I aimed to keep on building what I knew was home to me
home that was build all in my childhood,
where I learned that I was loved.

My home was, in fact, a person…just one person in this world
He was wise and he was loving,
He was strong and he was sweet
He called me his dear daughter
He protected me and loved me
Always took good care of me.

I traveled a long distance
Left my country and my mother tongue
Build new paths, yet no one ever told me
How empty this world could be
When the man that was my hero
Is no longer by my side.

And ever since the heavens came to reclaim him
I've been longing for a home
For a person to call my own
For a home while sailing solo
For an undying home at last.

Stanstead
Victoria J. Hamdi

Remains of Summer,
Linger into this fall evening.
Starched flower curtains,
hold guard-
Against the warm breeze.
In the dim kitchen,
Against dark brown paneling-I sit.
And pause.

This is where I remember,
You left me-
Unfinished.
Still eager to learn.
I understand enough,
But don't know everything.

My hands are young,
But rough from your lessons.
You taught me too well,
And you knew that.

Women of our line,
Don't stop working.
We are healers, workers and mothers.
Women who carry the families,
And move our traditions.
But we do not pause.
Tonight, for you-
I do.

Without you here,
My senses yearn for what is gone.
Footsteps-
The creaks of the house and

Smells of remedies.

But you are gone.
Gone my teacher,
My healer.
My nurturer.

I'm alone.
Our workspace so quiet now.

But I've paused for too long,
It's not enough.
To remember you,
Or let go of you.

To my feet,
There is much to do.

Fourteen Years
Michael Moats

It was fourteen years
after the death of their son.
A blink of an eye;
Yet, years of a torturous void.

Walking the city streets,
It was a beautiful night.
The stars could be seen,
in spite of the city lights.

A consistent hum of traffic,
subtly present during our traveling conversation.
The breeze seemed to blow
a sense of peace.

From seemingly nowhere to any observer,
but from a very unique place,
a known place in her heart and mind,
the pain burst forward.

Unable to continue walking
or entertain a seemingly empty conversation,
through barely audible words,
her tears spoke with clarity.

I used to walk these streets
praying for God to save him.
She had not been back,
since his stays at the nearby hospital.

Fourteen years.

I always wondered what I would feel.
It's bittersweet.

I mean, it wasn't all bad when we were here.
We had some really good times.

We laughed.

And the tears
began to fall again.
Standing silent,
making room for a mother's grief.

The courage it took
to return to this neighborhood,
to allow herself to cry
for her dead son.

Fourteen years.

It had been almost as long as he was alive.

The Undertaking
Beverly Magovern

Summer in the Sierra can linger well past Labor Day, after the trails have emptied. There remains a stillness broken only by the snap of grasshoppers vaulting from path to twig. Lizards bask on speckled boulders while dust rises in puffs around each step I take, to settle brown on my ankles. The kerchief at my neck is damp, and my boots send cascades of pebbles as I shin up slabs of granite burnished by glaciers, till I reach a glimpse of the lakes. Chewing at raisins tasting of sunscreen and sweat and sipping lukewarm Gatorade, I gaze down on fir and pine jostling at water's edge, slaking their thirst with the last of the snowmelt. The waters shadow over, and I glance skyward. Snagged on peaks, above me clouds marshal in anticipation. Hurriedly I hoist my pack and drop back to the trail continuing upwards. At 7200 feet I buckle over, planting my palms on my knees, my breath catching under the burden of bone and ash. At last I step from the path into the rock expanse where stone trinities delineate the half-mile clamber to the gnarled cedar of our summers. "Overlooking Echo Lakes," he had said. "There would be nice." The clouds rupture, and drops sting my arms and tattoo the granite. The chipmunks explode in a cartoon frenzy and evaporate among the rocks. Breaking faith with my promise, I scramble to lower elevation, inhaling the prickle of freshly charged air. From the urn in my pack I hear my father make the raspy clearing sound in his throat, just as he always used to do when there was something he wanted to say.

Again
Lisa Vallejos

A flower burst through
A crack in the concrete
Stretching tender limbs to the sun.

The sun broke through
The snow filled skies
Caressing the Earth with her gaze.

And I, aching with grief,
Tucked both memories in the gray
Pocket of my soul.

Today, I reached into my soul again
Places I hadn't touched for they were
Too tender to not bleed.

Those memories were the first to emerge
Like crumbled, dusty notes
Trapped in lost time capsule.

My mind cleared like the sky after rain
I finally understand
Everything dies and lives again.

Dandelion by Richard Bargdill

The Threshold
John Chavis

Don't go silently?
I went.
I've been doing that for...ever
Don't go silently.
I did go.
And now I must return.

I hesitate at the door.
Whatever is across that threshold-
it's better than what's here.
Better than cowardice, stagnation, stuckness.
I will go my own way.
Open the door.

Sometimes
Judith H. Montgomery

An indigo cloak clasped at her paper throat,
my mother is stepping

deep and deeper into a forest wing-lit with birds,
a basket of seeds

clutched in her hand. Once in a while, she
remembers

and scoops deep into the swirl—and gathers
a handful to sow

all about her, strewing the path with her time-
tested mix of dun

pearls of millet, of Ethiopian nyjer tiny as
rice, the richest black-

oil sunflower seeds—and so making a feast
under her feet, to delight

the rose-breasted house finches, arrow-tailed
swifts, her juncos,

her mourning doves calling *where are you
where are you* as they

alight, as they light her path into thickening
woods. Sometimes,

she stops, to consider the narrowing way—
to right and left, storm-

clocked nurse logs stitched with soaked sword-
fern and moss, straddled

by opportune alder. Ahead, a dim bramble
of brush. Sometimes,

my mother looks back, turns around, around,
slippered feet tentative

over awkward ground laced with uneven
root-wad and rock

under drifts of soft duff. A vine-maple's
reddened and

tumbling leaves brush her wrist, and she stops
to point out the flutter,

color and call of so many birds to my father,
although he is not

on the path she follows into the tangled
heart of the forest,

close and damp after rain. These woods—vines
and branches, holes and

encroaching thickets—hers alone, where he can
not follow . . . . Now streaking

the dusk, one cardinal flares, far from their New
England home—scarlet-

headed and cloaked, plump ensign who darts
in and out

of the cumulate dark, to light on her shoulder—
and she feels how she

flies under his heart, how she enters his heart,
and he hers.

She picks up the basket, steps on into twilight—
the cardinal weeping,

his red breast sweeping and lighting the one-
way one way.

First published in *Cave Wall* (nom. for Pushcart) 2013

Bitter Watch
Kat V. Rosemond

9/11 Anniversary Poem

The night falls hard
In this bitter dark watch
I keep in the gathering silence.

It is here
It has arrived
In my heart
In my guts
In my bones
The dawn of the dark day
Imminent

So heavy is the shadow
Of the memory of violent death
Dealt so senselessly
to the poor souls

Even to the innocent babies
Snuffing out their new pure light
They were bringing

From the heavens to the Earth
Their burned deformed bottles
Lay on the ground
Amongst charred pieces
Of the lives of all the lost
Pieces of bags
Burnt edged fragments
All cordoned
In a circle
In the green grass
Black and Grey
Stripped of purpose

While the horrified eyes
Of motionless sitting
Search and Rescue dogs
Stare over them
into the smoldering wound
In Pentagon's side

The structure bleeds
A constant stream
Of grey water
Fraught with pieces of debris
Mixed with charred flesh

Groans emanate
From the deepest recesses
Of my body and soul
As if groaning in the twists
And distortions
Of melted windows
Jagged hribar
Hanging debris

Smoke weaving tentacles around me
and up into the air
Cinging my nostrils
The smell…unspeakable

Dark are the hallways
Filled knee high with water
Offices now tombs
Watery graves
With marks of the number of dead
On broken doorways
Awaiting recovery
And their journeys
To their bereaved

I pass each with my crew
In solemn reverent silence
As we watch over their caregivers
Who will retrieve them
Carry them far
From this forsaken corner of darkness

Perhaps a piece of my soul
Died there that day
Forever with the dead

The wine in my hand now
Feels like my blood
That ran out of my broken heart
I try to drink it back in

Courage is the medicine
My trembling fingers grasp.
My tiny candle
Here in the dark
Longing to release
A long stifled scream

On Pain and Healing
Melinda Rothouse

Let the pain be your guide, they said.
So I opened my body and heart
to the curious sensations
of bones fractured, bruised and aching,
muscles clenching for dear life
to hold me upright--
keep me from succumbing once again
to the awful pull of gravity.

Some days the pain softened,
and I could move freely, make love,
even dance to the sweet sounds of gypsy jazz.
Other days my spine screamed in agony and
I simply could not attend to the basic necessities.
Found myself huddled
on the floor, in the pose of the child,
my nervous system frayed,
gasping for some reprieve.

But I discovered the pain was not so solid,
that my bones had become a barometer
of the cold front passing through,
the rains enveloping the earth,
of cruel words and tender acts of love,
all registering deeply within my marrow.

Walking the streets,
grateful for strong legs and supple flesh,
I drank in the vastness of the sky,
quivered with the cool caress of the wind
like never before.

Precious, precious gift, to be alive,
embodied within skeleton and tissue

that can sustain blunt trauma,
and yet heal, again to feel
the warm glow of sun on skin.

Falling Apart
Candice Hershman

The flowers are unwinding:
turning in upon themselves,
differentiated vivid
gone brown universal,
the spry of supple stillness
bending into brittle,
more still.
We did not know it,
but the flowers have always been
moving. Now,
they archive themselves
in the finest degree of slow;
such quiet, inward adagio
fossilizing into eternity.
The scent is timeless as
a newborn.

Once again, I
examine tuberose and iris
closely,
then turn,
ears snagged on a crackle
still waning in the fireplace.
Last night,
my son and I labored
on almond wood resistant to fire,
rapidly ripping the pages from
last year's daily calendar book,
once refined in black moleskin,
innards now used days feeding
the log's minutes.
The wood finally caught,
lambency creeping like worms,
flickering low rather than ablaze,

our invocation feeling both a small victory
and great failure.
I thought the fire would fast burn out.
This morning I see
nearly all of the largest log
is a pile of
ash,
no trace of orange ember,
yet the crackle utters
sporadically.

I thought of the time I
helped a man die:
In the hospice room,
angelic birth loomed like consciousness,
waiting to be penetrated,
wanting to be loved;
the same as the day
I received my firstborn.

I think of the last cadaver I'd seen,
just post-final heartbeat.
I could swear she wasn't
real-ly
dead.
At first I feared
she was trapped in decay,
in helpless pain
but for her look of peace.
Now I wonder
if heaven is
not minding our own
falling apart.

Alma
Victoria J. Hamdi

They say my land is not in drought.
    But dust blows across the barren plain.
Birds peck at what remains,
    If anything remains.

Morning comes as expected,
    And I stare across the land.
There is no movement.
There is no sound.

Earthworms turn the soil
    But nothing grows as Faith is planted.
Tractors sit asleep.
Workers check the earth for Hope once again.

I count the days,
    The hours,
        The minutes. All gone.

To the ground I kneel and let dirt slip through my fingers,
    Carried by the wind.
Hanging my head low,
    I cry.
In tears, I scream a prayer
    Painful for God to hear.
So many questions,
    And horrible pain without understanding.
 For I am a dead field-
    Alongside blossoming orchards.
Have I not attended my crops?
    Have I not planned my seasons?
There's blood in the dirt,
    And I'm not enough for this labor.

I pray continuously:
God, let this land bear fruit and not stay barren.
     Please give me the harvest in my dreams.
The wind blows hard and I get to my feet.
     Determined I scan the land one last time,
         Nothing.
    As I walk,
        The silence of the land cut.
    By the sound of life growing from the earth.
Closing my eyes, I turn my face to the sky.
And feel rain fall upon it,
     With the smell of freshness from the land.

Processing...
Emily Lasinsky

I hear grief and loss,
I experience grief and loss,
Just when I think grief is lost,
It finds a way back around.

Recent events pile high,
Groans of humanity flood the newspaper.
A woman badly injured, her child died,
Dare not ask, "What's next?"
Leaves me in fear of getting *the* call or text.

I try to see the good, be the good,
Pull back the heavy curtain,
Shed some light through the cloudy window, although so much
  remains uncertain.

I painted my future three years ago-a time when I *thought*
  everything was perfect.
The painting was not finished,
It has evolved, grown with me.
Doors close, but others eventually open.
I could close my eyes and my heart, but I choose to keep them
  open.
My experience is *not* for nothing.

I hear grief and loss,
I experience grief and loss,
And each time it comes around,
I'm steady...stronger somehow.
Feet planted firmly on the ground.

Blue
Amelia Isabel Torres

For Machelle.

I saw a blue balloon today
floating along the stratosphere —
caressing heaven's belly, batting
its glittering eye, intrinsically aware
of its place between the cosmos.

I saw a blue jay today
squawking down below our porch —
flitting among the branches, hopping
alongside the dry creek bed, content
in his handsome feathered frame.

I saw a blue bicycle and his sister today
racing each other through the park —
squealing in delight, wanting not
to be last, training wheels flying
as swift as wings.

I saw you everywhere today
coloring shirts and shoes and a dragonfly kite —
laughing behind graffiti, smiling across
the expansive Texas sky, your blue hair waving
in my memory.

Horse of Snow White
Jesse S. Moats

My wife rode away
On a horse of snow white,
And the things that I saw
Was a sheer awesome sight.
Seven angels rode escort,
As they sang sweet refrains;
My wife rode behind
As the Lord held the reins.
Swiftly they went
With the speed of gazelles;
The horses' muscles all flexed
As they swished their white tails.
Jesus spoke as they rode off
On that snowy white horse.
I'll be back for you,
After you've run your course.

I Stand
Shawn Rubin

I stand. Shocked and devastated. The blows of fate have violently shaken my view of the world, my self, the order and meaning of my life.

I stand. In sorrow, grief, confusion, inferiority, and self-blame. Emotions rage within me and color my world.

I stand. Pain impacts and batters my body. I sense the heaviness, tension, and dreadful foreboding. I stand disoriented, lost in my own skin.

I stand. At times constricted and suffocated, struggling for air and the expanse of freedom.

I stand. Reluctant to accept this undesirable reality.

I stand. Noticing my simultaneous mobilization and solidity of being.

I stand. Though I know not where, not how, not why, not when. I phase in and out of time. I enter one moment and exit months later.

I stand. Here and now. Now. Meeting this moment. It is only here that I can adjust my posture. It is only here that I may engage the effortless flow of intention and action.

I stand. Knowing that this moment and all moments must pass. Knowing that I, too, must pass.

I stand. Bearing witness to my pain. Allowing the depths of feeling and overwhelming loss to reside within me.

I stand. Observing my perpetual reactions, my shortness of sight. The well-worn path of my thoughts and actions leading in circles and dead-ends.

I stand. Distinguishing thought from emotion. Assuming responsibility for their separate content and quality of their combined power.

I stand. Relinquishing my defenses, receptive to the wider spectrum of existence. Walls come crumbling down. I surrender my illusions of control, safety, and privilege. Chaos and death await at the end of each animating breath.

I stand. Awakened to the folly of my narrow values, constructs, expectations, and wishes. I will the creation of new meanings as I make contact with a larger reality.

I stand. Discovering meanings in symbols and rituals that reflect my tenuous existence as well as my willful determination.

I stand. Between the paradoxical twins of life and death, conscious and unconscious, fight and surrender, belonging and loneliness.

I stand. Alone. Solitude, and its offering of protection, tranquility, and inner-attention, has become a cherished friend. Introspection serves as a guiding voice for inner yearnings.

I stand. Arms open to you as lifeline, nurturer, and receiver of my hurt. Your embrace comforts and reassures me.

I stand. In humbled awe of your composure and resilience through adversity. I learn from and take comfort in your strength.

I stand. Recognizing the limits of your soothing and my ultimate responsibility for healing myself.

I stand. Sensitized to your pain through the struggle of my own. I extend my hand to you, knowing your pain, and knowing your potential for overcoming this pain.

I stand. With a sense of mission in connections with others and purposes extending beyond my own needs.

I stand. Achieving a new understanding of fate, what has been and will be. The tragic is part of life, an obstacle to be encountered and overcome.

I stand. Knowing the wisdom of humility, surrender, and impermanence. I attune my perspective and values according to the discipline of these principles.

I stand. Immersed in a sense of belonging and communion with all sentient life and all of creation. The cycle of life and death is alive and I am alive in it.

I stand. Shaken but not annihilated, not defeated. I have danced with shadows and rejoiced in the light.

I stand. Alive, active, and centered amidst the spiraling mystery of possibility.

I stand. Unfolding and becoming, among the awesome dynamism of chaos and integration. My will is the driving force in forging a connected, loving, and enduring existence.

I stand. Resolute, engaged, and open to the challenge of the full spectrum of living.

Send-off
Robert A. Neimeyer

The dead linger around us,
stand at the shore
ready to push off
in their slow boats.
They finger the mooring line,
cast an eye to the sky
grey with rain. They feel
the ebb tide coming for them,
drawing them away
like forgetting.

They wait, patient as pilgrims,
for our thick hold to weaken,
arms to fall. They yearn to slip free
of the tight knot of our grief,
seek the silence beyond our piercing sobs.
They know in their bones
we will not lift the anchor,
hoist the sail. They bear the farewell
as a final duty.

We reach for their thin hands,
clutch their skirts, tug their sleeves.
We seek the refuge of their limp arms
as a ship steers toward harbor
in a storm. They hold our past
in their vacant eyes. Our future
is sealed behind their lips. We cannot bear
the endless present.

They sense the call to board their vessels
like the screech of distant gulls. They feel
the tremble in our fingers, hear
the gathering quiet

in our wracked gasps. They know
the months are doing their rhythmic work,
wearing us like waves. In the end
we will release them,
force a wan smile, raise an anxious palm

or join them in our time
to make the passage.

The Return of Spring
Paul T. P. Wong

Return after the Japanese tsunami

The cherry trees are budding
Their blossoms will be falling
When the swallows return
Will they find their homes?

Poetry Activities

Activity 1: My Journey With Loss
This activity is a continuation from the activity suggested prior to the introduction of the book. In the section, *Setting the Context*, you were encouraged to complete the following:

<u>Before reading this book -</u>

I thought of loss (any form) as:
I felt loss was:
I was:
Loss held:

Now that you have finished the book, complete the following:

Today, I think of loss as:
Today, I feel loss is:
Today I am:
Loss holds:

In the future, I think loss will:
In the future, I feel loss will:
My hope for future encounters with loss will be:
The future looks:

Today was my tomorrow.
Tomorrow will be my today.
Today my past meets my hopes.
Today, in spite of loss, I choose to:

Combine the previously completed section and the recently completed section into one poem. Do not make any adjustments or corrections at this time. Read it silently to yourself. Sit with any thoughts, feelings, or physical sensations that may arise. Listen...... If working with a group, read your poem out loud to your paired partner or entire group, based on how the group is arranged. If working on this alone, you may incorporate a friend, a family member, or a colleague to read this to you out loud. Make sure that you and your volunteer are aware that this can bring out strong emotional reactions by sharing in this manner. Whether working with a group or with a volunteer, notice your thoughts, feelings, and physical sensations. Take a moment to write them down, even if in a shorthand manner. This also allows the other(s) to sit with their reactions before sharing with you their experience(s). Others should be informed that their feedback should only include what they thought, felt, and their physical sensations, not critique as to form, content, flow, or preferences.

Activity 2: Needed or Not Needed
Divide into groups of 4-6 people, preferably through a random selection. Take turns choosing different poems from the book. Keep track as to not be redundant in selection. After a poem is selected by each participant, have each member read their poem aloud, allowing for at least 20-30 seconds of silence between each reading. Do not discuss the poems until after everyone has finished, and avoid debating the meaning or structure of the poems. The purpose of this activity is to collaboratively share individual and collective experiences with what is felt beyond the words, structure, or preferences. Use the following discussion points to guide the discussion:
1. What were the explicit needs, or literal needs, that you heard from the grieving?
2. What were the implicit needs, or meaningful needs beyond the words, that you heard from the grieving?
3. What feelings arise in each person while processing the needs of the grieving?
4. What are the commonly believed needs, or undesired needs, of the grieving that they are not asking for, explicitly or implicitly?
5. What feelings arise in each of you while processing the undesired needs of the grieving?

6. How do these stated needs and undesired needs conflict? What are possible consequences of these conflicts?
7. How might we be missing the mark in one's intent to support the grieving?

One question to always keep in mind: Who's needs are being met?

Activity 3: Hearing Differently
Divide into groups of 4-6 people, preferably through a random selection. Each member will write a poem expressing his or her loss (varied forms of loss likely). This can be in the form of rhyming, free prose, haiku, or anything that the author determines to be poetry. After all members have completed their writing, pass your poem to the person on your right. Choose someone to begin the readings. After the first reading, allow at least 20-30 seconds of silence, then group will share their experience of the poem (e.g., what they thought, emotionally felt, physically felt). Avoid debating the meaning or structure of the poems, and the feedback should not include critique of any kind. After everyone has had a chance to give feedback (every member does not need to give feedback each time), have the original author read the poem again. Allowing another 20-30 seconds of silence following this reading, have the group again reflect on their experiences, especially noting any differences they may have noticed within their mental, emotional, or physical reactions. The purpose of this activity is to collaboratively share individual and collective experiences about how grief is uniquely expressed and experienced. Use the following discussion points to guide further discussion:
1. What have you learned from this exercise?
2. How might this new insight change the way you support the grieving?
3. How might this new insight change how you approach your own grieving?

Activity 4: Writing in a Different Voice
One way of using poetry in the service of empathy is to attempt to write in the voice of another person. For this exercise, spend some time trying to get into the experience of someone who has experienced a loss or life transition and then attempt writing a poem in their voice. It is important to recognize that we can never know someone else's experience and this exercise is not intended to suggest that we can know someone else's experience through writing a poem in a different voice. However, the process of preparation as well as the process of writing can often bring unexpected insight. The preparation may involve reading stories, watching movies or documentaries, or listening closely to people speak about their experience. Engaging in these activities with the intent of writing in another's voice often changes the way one listens and sees.

This activity is an adaptation of an activity included in the book *Stay Awhile: Poetic Narratives on Multiculturalism and Diversity* by Louis Hoffman and Nathaniel Granger, Jr.

Activity 5: Changing Voices
Write the same poem in your voice at different times of your life. Although you could write about whatever theme you would like, it is often best to use a theme such as your self-identity or your spiritual identity. For example, you may begin writing a poem as best as you can in your own voice as an adolescent. You could revise this poem to your voice in college, then as a newly married person, as a parent, etc.

Alternatively, you could commit to working with one poem over time. In this approach, you would write a poem now and revisit it every few months or once a year and revise it, keeping the older versions of the poem.

A variation of this activity could be used with grieving or loss. Write a poem about a recent loss. Revisit this poem, making revisions, over time. It can be particularly helpful to write revisions around the times of significant events, such as anniversaries, holidays, or other special periods/activities that you shared with this person.

Activity 6: Journeying into Grief and Loss

Death, loss, and life transitions often feel overwhelming, particularly when we are resistant to allowing ourselves to experience them. Paradoxically, when we allow ourselves to journey into the experience it often changes the way we experience the accompanying emotions, such as grief, loss, sadness, and anxiety. This book can be a way to help people become more comfortable around grief, loss, and life transitions in general, or to journey into a particular experience of grief or loss.

If you read one poem from this book a day, it would take you over 2-months to complete. Even if you have already read the book once, we encourage you to make a commitment to read through this book once again at a slower pace. As you read through at this slower pace, try reading one poem a day. As you do this, here are a few suggestions to enhance and deepen this journey:

1. Read the same poem 2 or 3 times a day, including once at the beginning of the day and once right before going to bed. These times are important. Reading the poem in the morning can help you to be mindful of the meaning this poem can bring to you throughout the day. Also, your unconscious will continue to reflect upon the poem even as your consciousness is directed to your daily routine and responsibilities. You continue to process information at night in your sleep. Reading the poem again before bedtime primes your unconscious again to continue processing the poem.
2. In at least one of these readings, read the poem out loud.
3. With each reading, take at least 3-5 minutes to reflect upon the poem, its emotions, what it evokes in you, and what it might feel like to be the author or voice of the poem.

4. If you are using this activity to explore a particular loss or transition, try to journal for at least 5-10 minutes once a day after one of the readings of the poem. If the inspiration arises, allow the journaling to include your own poems.
5. If you have been experiencing feelings of overwhelming grief of sadness, it is recommended that you do this activity in conjunction with therapy or counselling.

This activity is an adaptation of an activity included in the book *Stay Awhile: Poetic Narratives on Multiculturalism and Diversity* by Louis Hoffman and Nathaniel Granger, Jr.

Activity 7: Images and Poetry

Gather a number of photographs of yourself across different periods of your life. Spend some time looking through these photographs, trying to get in touch with what your life felt like at these different periods. Use these photographs as a stimulus to lead into a poem.

You may also consider trying this same activity with photographs of someone you love, possibly someone who died or is no longer in your life. Sit with the photos and reflect upon your relationship, trying to remember the many emotions you had with this person as you let this serve as the inspiration for a poem.

Activity 8: Deathbed Poem

A common activity that people are asked to participate in is writing their own obituary. As a variant of this activity, consider writing a deathbed poem. Imagine looking ahead to your own impending death. Write a poem in this voice, imagining it to be the final poem you ever write.

This activity can be particularly poignant as part of a group activity where you can share your poems or experience of writing the poem.

Poetic Encounters Along the Path of Grief & Loss

Activity 9: Poetry Dialogue

The purpose of this activity is to stimulate a dialogue between two people or perspectives. This can be done individually, in a dyad, or in a group.

1. Individual Dialogue: If doing this as an individual activity, the person writing the poem will write poems from two different voices. For example, the person may write a poem to someone who has died and then write a response poem in the voice of the person who died. This can consist of two poems, or can be continued as a series of poems.

2. Dyad or Group: In a group setting, one person shares a poem and the other person or persons write a response to this poem. In the case of a death or a lost relationship, the response poem could be in the voice of the person who is being grieved. If two or more people are writing about the same loss, the response poems could be generated from different experiences of the loss. The response poems could also be the poet's own subjective response to the original poem. An example of a similar exercise in the current volume is the collection of four poems called "Sharing Grief."

About the Editors

Louis Hoffman, PhD, has been writing and presenting poetry for many years. His first edited poetry volume, *Stay Awhile: Poetic Narratives on Multiculturalism and Poetry*, was published earlier in 2015 with Nathaniel Granger, Jr. as the co-editor. He is a father, husband, and loving dog owner.

Dr. Hoffman is a licensed psychologist and a faculty member at Saybrook University, where he teaches the courses, "Poetry, Healing, and Growth" and "The Use of Poetry with Death, Loss, and Life Transitions." He is also the director of the Existential, Humanistic, and Transpersonal Psychology Specialization at Saybrook University and teaches courses on humanistic and existential therapy, international psychology, multicultural issues, and spirituality, as well as the courses on poetry.

Dr. Hoffman is active writing scholarship as well as poetry, and has a total of 6 books to his credit along with numerous journal articles and book chapters. He has served as the president of the Society of Humanistic Psychology. A co-founder of the Zhi Mian International Institute of Existential-Humanistic Psychology, he has been active in dialogues and trainings on existential psychology in China and Southeast Asia. You can find more out about his writing and scholarship at www.louis-hoffman.com.

First and foremost, Dr. Michael Moats describes himself as a father, a husband, and a friend. His passion as a clinical psychologist lies in working with clients who are learning to redefine their lives and create new meaning, especially those dealing with grief and loss in its many forms (i.e., death, divorce, job loss, recent move, natural disaster, war).

Michael was raised in a rural area, in which family and community were an important part of his cultural heritage.

Struggle, challenge, curiosity, and death were all experiences that would set him on a path that had not been understood, until later in his life. Michael would say that his knowledge of grief and loss has been heavily influenced by an experiential understanding, with a twist of theory for academic legitimacy. His greatest mentors have been hospice patients and their families, his family and friends that have died, and those friends, family, and colleagues that have navigated loss with a Zhi Mian attitude. He would not negate the importance of theory and intellectual knowledge concerning grief and loss, but he would argue that theory cannot touch the significance of having the courage to experientially engage the feelings of helplessness of another and accompany them without trying to fix it.

Dr. Moats recognizes that every instance of loss is new and is not competitive. The subjective experiences are heavily influenced by culture, experience, resiliency, spirituality, support, and meaning, which was a motivating factor for his research interests, including a qualitative, cross-cultural study (China and the US) that investigated meaning making and the lessons learned through loss. Additionally, he is a published poet and author of various book chapters and articles, as well as a co-founder of the Zhi Mian International Institute of Existential-Humanistic Psychology, promoting continued international dialogue and training to contribute to a more rounded perspective within the global, psychological community.

www.ingramcontent.com/pod-product-compliance
Lightning Source LLC
Chambersburg PA
CBHW050520170426

43201CB00013B/2031